As for Me
and
My House

As for Me and My House

Emma Lou Thayne

Bookcraft
Salt Lake City, Utah

Except where otherwise indicated, the poetry included in this book is by Emma Lou Thayne and is protected by copyright. That which has previously been published comes from the following sources:

"Knowing That Most Things Break," *Spaces in the Sage* (1971); "Repair," *Until Another Day for Butterflies* (1973); "Rip Off" and "Hold," *On Slim Unaccountable Bones* (1974)—published by Parliament Publishers, Salt Lake City.

"After the Wedding" and "The Building," *The Family Bond* (1974)—published by Nishan Grey, Salt Lake City.

Library of Congress Catalog Card Number: 89-85671
ISBN 0-88494-716-5

First Printing, 1989

Printed in the United States of America

To the dears who have been part of me and my house

Contents

Acknowledgments

For encouragement, criticism, patience and direction, I would like to thank readers and editors Lowell and Merle Bennion, William and Dorothy Stafford, Barbara Duree, Lavina Fielding Anderson, DeAnn Evans, Edith Shepherd, Shauna Lloyd, and Elizabeth Haglund. For a place to work, Peggy Thomas.

For being the source, I am grateful to my family, Mel; Becky and Paul, Nicky, Richard and Michael; Rinda and Jim, James, Katie and Liska; Shelley and "P," Grace, Coulson and Eric; Dinny and Mike, Brittany and Warner; Megan and Ed and Daniel.

And, of course, Mother, Father and Grandma, who stay part of everything.

Foreword

The title of this book doesn't begin to reveal its depth and richness. Emma Lou Thayne transforms the drudgery of housework into something creative and well worth doing. She makes fun projects out of humdrum experiences. She brings a zest to the home which makes it an inviting place to enter.

References to housekeeping and home maintenance are incidental to life lived in her house. This work is the author's autobiography of life lived with her family. She tells in an honest, graphic way her relations with her mother, father, grandmother, brothers, husband, five daughters, grandchildren, and friends.

Gifted with a poet's sensitivity and intuition, she finds meaning in commonplace experiences as well as in the joys and tragedies of life. She meets life with curiosity and wonder and transforms it in the image of her own mind and heart. She has had her share of accidents and suffering but has met them with courage and faith and overcome them with gratitude.

She writes beautifully with a remarkable command of language. The writing holds one's attention. This is a book for men as well as women to enjoy.

LOWELL L. BENNION

Introduction

Eight years ago, the *Ensign* asked me to write an article about housekeeping/homemaking. I was intrigued. I wrote my story and found it to be many stories. For twenty-five years, I had grown up in a home with a grandmother, a mother, a father, and three brothers; after that I had been married to the same man for nearly forty years, thirty of them spent in the home we still live in, fifteen of those years with my widowed mother living in a wing built for her. I had been mother to five daughters, had become matriarch to a family of twenty-four—and growing—now spread over three states.

And all the time I had lived as much outside my home as in, as a teacher, writer, skier, board and committee member, tennis player, lover of the many and the much that held and occupied me. Life anywhere had never been simple. Nor had it been free of frustration, grief, depletion, and concern. But it had been full —and happy.

When I was in my thirties with a household of five little children under ten, I read Ann Morrow Lindbergh's *Gift from the Sea* and dreamed of time to meditate, time to impose meaning on all that was going on in my life. Not until I was past half a hundred did I have the time, and that assignment by the *Ensign* triggered the impetus to examine specifically how I felt about home and its makings.

I loved the chance. The one story, stretching over almost a decade and sandwiched between hundreds of other writings, turned into sixteen meditations on housekeeping and homemaking.

Nothing is more personal than the house, the home, the place that I live in. Nothing more reflects my sense of the world or my regard for what is important. Through it stream my passions, my people, my phases, and my philosophies. Into it I allow the programs, the pages, the food, the habits that persuade my days and occupy my nights. It is my shelter, the husk of me. In it I am warm and cold, from happy to sad, thoughtful or automatic, active and passive, sometimes touched by the divine, always subject to being human.

What happens behind that front door can be up for speculation but never known by anyone outside it. It is my domain.

How I live in it counts, not only to me and mine but also to others who are beneficiaries, either directly or indirectly, of the good or ill will that derives therefrom. Every household, like every person, makes a difference. And everyone does it differently, the keeping of that house. The statement "as for me and my house, we will serve the Lord" (Joshua 24:15) is a voiced assertion of one overriding aspect of the keeping. There can be many others.

This book is simply a telling of some of the keeping that has made it a challenging, changing, often depleting, more often satisfying way of living for me.

1

On Keeping My House

I've lived in the same house for nearly thirty years—most of my married life. I've done a lot of growing up there with Mel, a seldom-there but devoted realtor husband and father, and with our five daughters—Becky, Rinda, Shelley, Dinny, and Megan. What a time we've had! And much of that is now part of a house grown out of itself as "Mel's Belles" have gone off on their own.

A lot of housekeeping happened in those thirty years. A lot still does—as it does in the homes of our grown daughters, all of them married and involved in the same good and demanding life, with now a total of thirteen children—and counting—among them.

I like now, these "later years," having a house stay clean for more than five minutes, having fun with my grandchildren and not having to get them ready to go, not trying to settle them in at night, not ever having to be pregnant again—having my daughters do all that for me—and having choices about getting up and going to bed and what I do in between. But I liked that housekeeping, still do, maybe because it's one of the things I do best, thanks to the training I got in the home where I grew up. But how I choose to do it is not all traditionally as I was brought up to do.

I learned dusting and polishing from a meticulous and home-body mother, Grace Richards Warner, whose mothering I've revered and written about in books, in stories, in a novel—*With Love, Mother,* "Mother Killed the Rattlesnakes," *Never Past the Gate.* Her keeping a home and keeping a house were two different things. From the time I was twelve I cooked for her, my three brothers, and my father, Homer "Pug" Warner, in a home full of laughter and love—and fastidious order. Mother taught me early how to miter sheet corners in making a bed, to fold linen exactly square, to dust corners without "soiling" the wall, to leave a bath-room spotless and ringless after every ablution.

She taught me how to polish silver, "soda" an icebox (later a fridge), clean ashes from a fireplace, set a perfect formal table, iron a shirt—starched!—in fifteen minutes, darn a sock or sometimes a silk stocking, have a pot roast and peach cobbler steeping in their juices before Sunday School and ready after, with potatoes mashed without a lump, gravy smooth as water over a spillway. She taught me to make a mustard plaster and turkey dressing, to write poems to go with candles for a birthday.

She kneaded seven loaves of bread twice a week, teaching me to love the smell of yeast and the feel of dough—and always to be a "neat cook," clearing and cleaning up almost before ingredients made it to the pan. Every fall I peeled while she bottled three hun-dred quarts of fruit, ladling chili sauce or grape conserve, pungent and steaming, onto melted butter seeping into the end piece of bread just out of the oven.

Saturday mornings were sacred. Dirty or not, every corner of the living room, the kitchen, the dining room, and every bedroom was swept, vacuumed, dusted, fluffed, and polished. The bathroom —we had only one for seven of us, with a makeshift shower in the basement for my brothers—was polished like a crystal ball. Spring housecleaning lasted the entire week of spring vacation. The boys and Father scrubbed the floors and rugs with squishy melted H&H soap and cleaned the walls with tangy-smelling pink dough that turned streaked black, while I stretched the curtains on prickly frames by the radiator and washed with ammonia, inside and out, the eighty-four leaded panes in each of three arched windows in the living room.

Luckily, fun was built into our days. We worked hard so we could play hard, both Mother and Father being believers in picnics and ball games (with me throwing too), bonfires and sleigh riding.

I was a happy, tomboy girl, with mostly tranquil acceptance of my role as female furnisher of clean clothes, neat rooms, made beds, and tasty, plentiful, and parsley-attractive meals for my beloved father and brothers, whose appreciation was rich with thank-yous and with pride in me as adoring provider of the quality of what they ate and wore and slept in. In the compliant upheaval of the forties, of course I would marry someone as loving as they and live happily ever after, perpetuating the myth: housekeeping + homemaking = a shiny, full life. That's what the women in my family did. That's what my friends did. That's what I (who had a hope chest at age five) grew up planning to do.

But I also saw the ways of my grandmother, Emma Louise Stayner Richards, widow of my grandfather Dr. Stephen L. He died before I was born and she lived with us, had earlier taught Mother as Mother taught me, with love, energy, and attention to detail. Each of them, though, moved on from full-scale housekeeping to mostly being consultant and matriarch to families who remember them both more for their wisdom and humor than for cleaning and cooking. Those tasks were done by others. In my growing up, I watched them delegate even as I was included in the delegation. Until I was twelve, we had different girls from rural towns live with us for board and room and five dollars a week to learn my mother's gentle attentions to a house and to us, with Thursdays and Sundays off to shop for mostly a husband. These girls became part of the family, were loving friends to us as well as of course full-time help for Mother and Grandma. But after I was twelve the girls were gone, and the delegating was pretty much to me.

By the time I was out of high school, I longed for a Christmas or summer job like the jobs my friends had, especially something that I could go away for that would make me feel like a grown-up on my own, actually earning a paycheck. Generous as they always were with me in every way, Mother and Father made sure I knew I was loved and that I had means to match the abundance of my interests, but my "work" was at home, keeping the house that I so loved and so wanted to move on from. I did so only when I married. And then into another home to keep.

When my father died at age fifty-nine, Mother, on much urging, moved into her wing of the house, an addition she built with Mel and me and our three very little girls, with the first of two more on the way. Like Grandma, she would be a part of our home but not be a built-in though glorified baby-sitter. She had done that. It was time for her to be herself, with her easel up in her sitting room and the big black leather rocker ready for callers.

My grandmother had been a guest at our table, invited from her upstairs rooms, rooms that we children were in turn invited to visit. She was my idol, my pal, a reader of books and taker of trips, a member of the Friendship Circle, the Author's Club, and a hostess for friends who would plan week-long bridge and Rook parties at her mountain cabin—and she was not my supervisor or disciplinarian. I dreamed of one day going off with her and her huge trunk on the Union Pacific to visit the place near the beach in Santa Barbara where she lived for three winter months. She read with me, listened to my stories, and praised the special "diabetic" muffins I made when I was eleven to take to her bed the year she lay dying of cancer. She let me learn the joy of doing for her, as part of the not-always-joyful doing for the house.

I wanted her life, but I didn't want to wait until I was seventy-five to have it. I wanted a house that shone like Mother's, but I didn't want to give my life to it. Mother's scrupulous housekeeping became for me my "oblique" style.

Mother had stayed home most of my childhood, part of a generation that left only for sewing club every other Friday, had her groceries delivered from the Sugar House Merc, made every outfit I ever wore—and had me try each one on, it seemed, at least two hundred times. Like every one of her friends, she had no thought for or need of a job away from home, let alone of activity that would require running. Though her hands were never still, the most active things I remember her doing outside were drawing a marble ring in the hard dirt that splotched our back lawn and killing those rattlesnakes that dared the premises at the cabin. She was home. And in the house. Even the girls who lived with us never tended us.

When I became a homemaker I, like most of my generation, brought in sitters. As a realtor, Mel was on call like a doctor, and in addition he taught classes two nights a week to augment the potential and the irregular income of a salesman. I too was never without a class to teach in the ward or part-time at the university, and I loved being outdoors and running on a court or hiking with my family and friends even more at fifty than I had at fifteen. Much had changed since Mother and Grandma raised their families.

From the time of my childhood, my generation had seen the coming of airplanes, toasters that pop, disposals, a gas furnace, automatic water heaters, washing machines, and dishwashers. We had grown into frozen foods, plastic, detergents, stainless steel, hi-fi and then stereo, and milk in cartons in supermarkets—a far cry from Fisher Dairy bottles with long necks, bottles delivered to our back porch to raise their caps with frozen cream to have on hot oatmeal. Into our lives came Cheerios, nylon, polyester, permanent press, ballpoint pens, electric blankets, tranquilizers, and pants and shorts on women. Mother never wore either, but maintained herself as a "lady" in her white gloves and hat until she died at the age of seventy-six in 1972. Antibiotics had replaced mustard plasters, turkey dressing could be everyday stir-fry, and coal-black walls and nostrils, monkey stoves, and depression gardens of bridal wreath and castor beans had faded long before the arrival of instant breakfasts and TV dinners, both of course scorned by Mother and used only guiltily by me. Life was different. But with Mother, the same. Yet in writing this book, in meditating on our different ways of doing, I realize how much of me continues to be what she so thoroughly inculcated during those years of change and stasis.

Mother saw me operate sometimes with exasperation and exhaustion but with the undercurrent of satisfaction, yes, even joy, in doing what I had learned and what I mostly loved to do now

that I was on my own. I worked for and with a house full of people
I loved, trying for a clean house, with meals on the table or bar
pretty much on time—her meals not hard to serve in her little
kitchen where she preferred to eat apart from the hubbub of our
growing up. Eight plates instead of seven? Why not? The only complication being that her day—at my age now!—was sometimes
starting as mine was ending, her timing geared to a clock reset by
the stage of life she was in. While a lot of rush and urgency of
babies and then teenagers seemed ultimately manageable to me,
fun in fact, life in our house could be confusing to Mother, who
was used to quiet: children in bathtub frolics; a family noisy and
busy, sometimes with but mostly without TV; neighborhood
friends in and out; work parties on Saturday morning as expected
as kittens born in a bedroom closet. But also I was on the go, involved in teaching English part-time at the University; active in
the Mormon church and on the General Board of its youth program, the Young Women's Mutual Improvement Association
(YWMIA); planning, working, traveling for it (my children later
told me they resented my being gone sometimes forty hours a week
on Church work much more than the four I was gone teaching);
and also traveling with my husband to his real estate conventions;
playing tennis; skiing with him and the family; and keeping in
touch with fascinating friends. Independent as Mother wanted to
be, driving her car until almost her last day, still it was often far
from easy for her to watch my accommodations to the kind of
housekeeping I felt a place deserved. I always thought I simply grew
up different from what she expected. It was not until she was dying
that I really knew.

And now I was losing her, my Grace, my pillar, my
soft, soft lady with the lamp. I leaned close to her, con-
cerned that she hear, as she always had, my concern. I'd
been a daughter different by far from the one I'd always imagined her wanting—a needlepoint, demure daughter more
like her than my athletic, involved father. We'd joked about
it before, but now I said, "Mother, I know you've always
wished I'd take a gentler horse."

She opened her brown eyes, flashing in dark circled settings, squeezed my hand harder, and said, "No. I've always loved you on the wild one." (*With Love, Mother* [Salt Lake City: Deseret Book, 1975], pp. 8–9.)

Just so, even as her accommodation to my keeping of a house was sometimes stressful to both of us, being together in the growing was like getting to live a part of our lives over again. I rather think she knew it had to be done my way as well as hers. And that was all right. Just as it must be for me as I see my daughters growing into their own ways of doing and becoming.

When I was four, eight, ten, I loved putting my dolls—as many as sixteen—to bed every night in my playhouse, formerly the coal room in the basement. Grandma had men take a jackhammer to the coal chute and put in a window for my "family." But never did I expect, nor did anyone else, that I would still be there at fourteen or at twenty bathing the same dolls and singing "rock-a-bye" to them every night. Instead, by then that room had been stuccoed and converted into a makeshift study. There my old Remington typewriter rattled off term papers into the night on Father's cast-off desk. Before that, my brother Homer had used it to dissect his medical-school cats, so close to the furnace that formaldehyde slept with us in our bedrooms two stories up. My brother Rick strung tennis rackets there, and Gill continued studying his scriptures there at twenty-one after his two-year self-supported proselytizing mission for our church.

My brothers all moved on, I moved on. None of them, much alike as they continue to be in basics, could ever trade jobs with each other. Any more than I could with the ways of their wives, Kay, Marian, and Nedra, the sisters in my adulthood that I had longed for while growing up. And that's pretty wonderful. We were all married in the Salt Lake Temple, three of us in the same year. We have children and now grandchildren close to the same ages, even live only blocks apart. But how we do our homes, my brothers and their partners, Mel and I, has changed as we've lived those years as close as any extended family ever could hope to be.

This small book muses, in sixteen essays and interspersed poems, about my changes, about housekeeping and homemaking —about living—about me and my house, and about how it has become only one of the places where I feel at home.

House

Even God cannot take my life back
once I have turned it over day by day.
Any more than I can call to the ghosts
in the pictures, Return! Come home!

And you, House, haunt of what we came
around to, you deliberately ushered us out
changed, but always expecting
your bounty to be the same.

And so I will keep you, give only
what boards and mortar deserve,
saving old tastes of you, the intimate
dashes of salt in stew and butter in

thickening, and the unempty wisdom
of a place too recently full, now rightly lean.
I need you as I need my skin: Not to contain me,
but to make me possible at all.

2

On Mattering

We all need to matter—to someone else, to a project, to a day, to ourselves, to God. Maybe that's why keeping a home can be both satisfying, if I matter in it, or stultifying, diminishing, and defeating if I don't.

In my best moments, I can feel that what I do as a homemaker is to handle life, to be at the core of mattering. In my worst times, I can feel that what I do as a housekeeper is to handle mess and confusion—apart from life, shut off, repetitious, mundane, anything but mattering. But if I do it obliquely, housework can be background to whatever I choose to let matter most.

And I must remember that what matters most to me may not be what matters most to anyone else. The secret is to pay attention to what does. I may be perfectly comfortable and totally involved in a visit with a friend even as I dust a lamp or pluck off old geraniums, while that friend may have no need to do anything but sit and give full attention to what we're saying. "Jobs" become my physical outlet for what is really occupying me—people and ideas.

Here's a log of a housekeeping/homemaking day on a Monday morning in October when we were down to four: Mel and I, twenty-one-year-old Dinny, and high school junior Megan—a log that shows what mattered most to me on that particular day and what I felt made me matter to me or to anyone else.

7:40 A.M. While making the bed together, Mel and I talk over the day—how he can keep his blood pressure down, his real estate sales up—and how he can manage four appointments before lunch. He gulps his cranberry juice on his way to the door and says interest rates will hit an all-time high and buyers will never find a decent loan to buy anything.

While I let that wonderful fact sink in, I move from what might be despondency to the patio where fall demands my attention. I sweep up the golden leaves and punch them into bags, almost tasting the brittle curl, the tang, and the final pleasure of the gathering. I run my hands through the crunch, stirring like a squirrel, feeling muted, winterized. The old geraniums are shriveling. I yank gently, combining the smell of ripe roots and damp earth with the mint that I pull to set it off.

By then it's cold. My fingers blaze, my nose drips. I pause to admire, remember all the summer meals on the patio, then drape plastic over the huge tile table I made all those years ago out of a plywood Ping-Pong table and unused floor tiles from the basement bath. I hammer tacks to hold the covering snug. The yard is tucked into its leavings, spare and ready.

Going back into the warm kitchen, I ask myself almost absently, What did he say that prime rate was?

8:00 A.M. Our daughter Becky is on the phone. Four-year-old Richard has been throwing up all night and has a fever. First grader Nicky has dropped the newly spayed cat. It's hemorrhaging and he's asking for Band-Aids. And the stained glass mirror she's working on for her mother-in-law's Christmas has just crashed on both Nicky and the cat. Oh, Becky, oh, Hon, I think. I say, "I know. It sounds awful."

Miles from the disasters, I work through the shared pain. I let out the long cord on the phone in the bedroom and begin to attack the bathroom, the tub, wash down the walls, the phone squeezed on my shoulder by its new rubber rest. It is my private catharsis. The tile never looked so shiny, I tell myself, glad we chose the corn-yellow twenty-four years ago. But oh, I ache for what's happening in that other household.

I say, "Let me talk to Nicky. Nicky?" I finish brushing the toilet bowl. "Oh, Sweetie—your kitty. What a sadness." I feel it behind my eyes. "But your mommy says she'll be OK." He is crying. I want to hold him, but at the imposed distance I try diversion instead. "Things heal—they get better. They usually can get fixed . . . like I'm just admiring the great job you and I did refinishing this old toilet seat in our bathroom, the seat that was broken."

I wince as I think of the poor cat's troubles and Nicky's hurting, and run my hand over the grained satin feel of the repaired and refinished oak toilet lid. "We'll all think of your kitty and hope she gets well. It makes me feel sad. But remember how you helped me sand this wood so smooth we thought it was like a pebble from the bottom of the creek? Well, the stain came out just right. You'll love how it looks. That's how healing can work, you know. When you come for your haircut you'll be really surprised." He asks if Richard will be surprised too, " 'Cause right now he's asleep in front of the toilet at our house and likes it better than bed." Even in calamity, Nicky's description of Richard has made me smile. And think of his mother, Becky. I remember the frazzled days with five little girls under ten, when mayhem erupted in any corner like leaves in a whirlwind. I ask Becky, "How high was his fever? Have you tried a lukewarm bath yet? Oh, give them both a squeeze from me—and one for you too, Hon. You must be so frayed. What a morning!" I can feel it all, how it would be in person. I send huge hugs over the phone as I rub the cloth across the slick top of the seat.

8:39 A.M. A man from a magazine calls to talk about poetry, an interesting man, but with time to wonder at 8:40 A.M.? I go to the utility room and plug in the phone in a place where I can reach to sort and fold. The load just out smells of Bounce. It works, I think. I'm a living commercial! I remember how precise the hanging had to be in my girlhood, one sock, one shoulder, then another and another, ghosting up the neighborhood and coming in breathy as morning in the canyon.

Meanwhile, the piles of folding grow. Three out of six socks don't match. One has a hole. Remember when you darned? I think. You could make that hole a cross-stitch flat and tight as linen.

We are talking poetry and metaphor as I try to figure how to structure the load of clothes firmly enough to make it to drawers in one trip, leaving what has to be ironed. Mending is like a poem, I think. Maybe I even said it. The hole, the ragged edges, the pulling together not tight enough to pucker, thoroughly enough to hold, smoothly enough to make a difference without showing.

Then we are into a discussion of form and function, just where we wanted to be. And the clothes are on their way to drawers and closets, another phone cord spiraling behind me.

9:00 A.M. Our daughter Dinny, about to graduate to teaching, is up from her early desk and asking about her grammar midterm on modals and complementary nominative clauses or something— all with new names. While we talk, we pull some fresh sheets from the stack of laundry and go to her room. The unmade bed is easy to strip. Over the corners we slip the new sheets smelling of the un- wrapped Yardley soap in the linen cupboard. They tighten out their own foldings and the pillows drop into their crisp cases under our chins like adjectives under nouns on a diagram. "Mrs. Shep- herd in seventh grade at Irving had us do it this way. Simple," I say, "and fun," drawing lines and connections on her notebook by the bed. She nods, smiles that she understands. I know that she will one day teach it herself.

Neat, I think. Explainable as the comfort of a nighttime head on the newly changed pouf of a pillow. Housework, homework. All in the camaraderie of changing a bed while we figure out some ways, together.

9:36 A.M. A friend, seventy-five years old, is on the phone, stricken. The vigor of her magic fingers that have massaged health into generations of us and my surgeried back to working order, has been lost to hepatitis. She will have to go into a nursing home. I can't stand it. "Oh, my sweet Leda," I say to her, "you must be so grieved and worried. But we'll figure it out. Do you know how you've rescued me with your touch over the years?"

While we talk I remember the oppressive smell of mopped-up urine in the institution we visited last Christmas. I remember how she always washed and washed those strong hands with care and concentration, preparing her tools. How can she put them to use now? The calls need to be made.

In the sadness of making arrangements, I am saved by letting the kitchen happen. Blender for breakfast eggnog away. Hot water running off slick dishes from cereal. Meat browned for soup. An onion with its white rounds parting like starched collars. Celery. Bay leaf. Basil. Air full of what will be.

I remember the back surgery that brought Leda to me and I remember being in bed for four months feeling anything but useful, wanting not much more than to be able to put on a meal, to "keep" the house, to not be waited on. I ask about location, make a note to find out what rights she will be giving up as we apply for Medicaid. The pained wondering softens in the redolence of a kitchen and the right to prepare, the blessed right to be part of the process of making a home.

10:10 A.M. A talk for tomorrow has to be wrought. In the woe of thinking, Why didn't I put it together sometime before today? I head for the study with long-handled duster in one hand for the stair edges and a load of empty bottles and apple juice for the fruit room in the other.

On my way back I take a quick run around the playroom tile with the floor duster. Under the Ping-Pong table, the couch, in front of the fireplace. The dear old fittings take me along as I dust them—the coffee table made from a power company wire spool and painted blue like the Ping-Pong table to match the Oriental rug bought from Deseret Industries for $8 after it covered a stage for a June conference program (how many years ago?). The piano needs attention too. Dusting, I think, Father, how about one time through your song, "Danny Boy"? My whole repertoire, that one song, one I can't interrupt by thinking about how it's still happening or it will be lost. The keys feel good, as they did when I learned it for him when I was ten. My voice sounds bad, as always, but I sing very low, "And if you come, and maybe find me dying, or even dead, for dead I well may be." And there is the idea for the talk. About time. Its preciousness. I find myself in the study with the elixir of a notion about to take shape. Off the shelves, out of the file drawers, up from the scrapbooks, the feeling-into, the filling-out of an idea. Between writing parts of the outline, feeling totally absorbed in what is finding itself inside my head, I take my duster—luckily taller than I could reach—and "doodle" with it on the shutters and bookshelves.

Just before the conclusion, as I struggle for its coming, I take a slow run with the duster over the clear plastic protector that lets my high-backed rolling chair, discarded from Mel's old office, run where it will. That's it! I tell myself. End with the trade-offs of the mixture, the dulling, the shining of the moment. Housework has done it again.

Noon. Our third son-in-law, "P," husband of Shelley, drops by with our first granddaughter, Grace, to get a haircut and give a physical therapist's eye to my recuperating shoulder. He has tired eyes and his smile says he has worked sixty hours on the job and forty on building their house this week.

Sweeping up the clippings from his hair and hers is the most fun eighteen-month-old Grace has had all day. The fine light brown wisps fall like fringed confetti into the tall basket. She sorts it, lets it go between her tiny fingers.

Then, upstairs, she brings her dolly to sit beside me with both hers and the doll's feet dangling in the sink so she can help me wash carrots for the soup while the tall daddy with the jagged hair sleeps on the couch. I think, This is life eternal; this is being home. No wonder Mother loved it when any of us would take a nap at her house.

Grace and I get out the watercolors, and while I use the thick brown to cover up the white exposures of cording around the soft old sofa cushions that no one wants to have replaced, she paints stars and hearts on the table and pours the water on Pippin, who yips and hides behind her chair. I remember why doing a thing once was all right, why cleaning up after never was. Why a grand-child could get by with a whole bunch.

1:24 P.M. I want to get a letter off to daughter Rinda and her husband Jim in Dallas before the postman comes at 2:00. And the bank deposit. And the phone bill. And, oops, the reorder on salt, the answer to the questionnaire, the reference letter for a friend for graduate school, the thank-yous for the Xeroxed article, for the dinner last week, for the book last month.

"Dear Rinda and Jim," I begin. "You pros would have laughed seeing us try to take our pulse rates while riding the rented exer-cycle." Not yet quite focused, I turn to the file labeled "Business" and fill out a deposit slip while I think, I miss you and your little James and Katie as if someone had poured vinegar on a burn.

I give robot attention to paying bills, filing miscellany, collect-ing myself. Thinking of people I love to say thank you to allows my gradual return to writing the letter, the concentration it per-suades—as if the missing pair were here talking with me late at night in the study that then was in a very dark corner of the storage room. Now I can look out the window of the room that was Shelley's before she was married, and see ivy and honeysuckle, snow and sunsets in clouds. "How is the asthma, Rin? I hope this is a time when Texas and dryness are better than Utah and dryness. We need moisture to clear out the air and our psyches. Like you always could do with your always learning something new. Even more, we need you and your crazy pampering of us all. How will it be when Jim's training is over and you get to be people in the real world? Maybe even back here? Wow! In the meantime, we'll have that visit in March. Tell James and Katie to figure which bed I'll sleep in which night."

Three pages later, the letter finished, I think, Lunch. I forgot it. Good. Even in dieting, oblique is best. Maybe I can make up for nonstop caloric catastrophe yesterday, Sunday, the usual disaster on the scales. Being in the kitchen preparing the big dinner is like being an alcoholic in a brewery. I've lost a thousand pounds—the same five every week. The ups, the downs in everything. But, so? They compensate for each other.

2:00 P.M. Daughter Megan, off early this morning for Pep Club, will be home from school at 2:30. We've reserved a court for 3:00. I struggle into tennis clothes, balancing the phone on my shoulder, calling first to verify the court time, which I forgot to do at 7:30, then to ask a brother if we're getting together this Sunday with the family. Remember when Mother and Father were here, I think, always just coming home from somewhere with stories and little mementoes and the big, broad look at things? How I loved them, love them. But Mother's keeping house! So ticky, so constantly doing something. So never able to sit down and just be. Always had to have her hands busy.

Hey, I think, who am I kidding? I am my mother's daughter. Different jobs maybe, different approach. But I relish the joy in the shine exactly as she did and with hands that like not to stop. Amazing! It's just that I like working through more than one thing at a time. Obliquely. Every kind of work a meditation. Maybe in the same way a poet is said to be someone who likes to say more than one thing at once. It was even more necessary when I had a household swirling about me, me wheeling about in the noise, the repetition, the constant accompaniment, the day always running out before the jobs to be done. Mother, were you always awash in ideas even as you seemed so one-directional? I'm grateful that you taught me what you did. You made little things matter, even as I discarded your seeming to make them matter too much. We grow into our tasks, our way of life, just as our skin grows about us. Habit and wrinkles. Soft. Not too bad.

So goes the day. A rare one, mostly spent at home. Actually a not bad morning and afternoon with their comfortable calms in the eye of the hurricane. Of course, nothing is really finished. That's keeping a house, holding a household.

But, I think, today it mattered—obliquely. The jobs are done and I can't even remember doing them. Only that I liked it—a lot. It's the people, not the jobs, that stay. I must remember: I can endure enormous stress or enjoy generous contentment if I feel that what I am doing matters.

About Time

Each of us wants to be friends with time,
comfortable waiting for toast to pop,

pleased to pull at the garden knowing
no season is going off without us.

The trick is to find out
whether a minute is worth more

crammed or empty.
And, either way, to get on with it.

3

On Doing Mother's Curtains

Strange thing, this habit of housekeeping, especially my mother's kind of housekeeping. I can put it away for a time, but invariably it sneaks up on me and takes over.

Take one morning, for instance. When I was fifty-five and skiing with two of my speedy daughters on a hard-packed ridge, I suddenly thought, Hey, kid, you're going a hundred and fifty miles an hour! So of course I crossed my skis and spilled down the mountain—on my shoulder. My right arm had been out of commission since then for the better—or should I say worse?—part of eight months with a dislocating shoulder and a carpal tunnel numbness in the hand. Not big, the inconvenience, but enough to keep me saving the arm up for the really important, like throwing a football to a four-year-old grandson or splitting some firewood for the canyon stove or holding onto a pen or a spoon or a hand or a tennis racket. Somehow, things like the curtains in our bedroom were left to hang.

But during the time I had to spend in bed through the distinctly different weeks after surgery, I had noticed those curtains! Even past the head of a visitor or the rim of a book, they flapped over my conscience. Healing, I got up and out, expecting to escape their indictment. Instead, they sagged, slimpsy, as Mother would say, soiled, on their rods now exposed by the mute tongues of what was once starched embroidery on elegant voile.

These curtains had been my mother's favorite demonstration of domesticity during her fifteen years of living in this wing of our house. Once each year she performed her rite of spring—washing them by hand, blueing and starching and ironing them, a thick-folded sheet between them and the board so that the embroidery stood out like an engraved announcement of fastidious caring.

Now up from my bed, arm functioning, I gave in. I took the curtains rambunctiously, spontaneously to task. I performed the same ceremonies, Mother, only this time in December. I even moved three layers of supplies from the top shelf of the utility room cupboard to find Mrs. Stewart's Liquid Blueing and Kingsford's Starch. I dipped and spun and dried your curtains with the touch I would give to a baby. Ironing took me twelve minutes per curtain, seventy-two minutes for six.

A not bad concession to ritual. More than work, it was celebration.

Celebrating is sometimes what work can become. As Grandma said, "Dearie, work. When you're troubled, work. When you're happy, celebrate having worked."

So I do. Like my work with the curtains. She knew the great exorcising in the physical, the mind running like a river with twenty accesses to the sea, the spirit coming afloat with the buoying of each managed task. My arm was celebrating its healing. My universe was coming to order.

Blessed be the smoothness, the starchedness, the fragile perfection, I thought. Over how much else in my life do I have such control? And blessed be the time to press out a thousand wrinkles in the head and heart, the care and smoothing out of lives so complex, ironing so simple. Under the iron the steam does good things. It moistens and creases and goes away having done right by everything.

In a world of wash and wear, Mother's system is as antiquated as her white-glove-and-hat sallying into the world. Of course I love the freedom of a no-iron day in which even wrinkles are acceptable, yes, mostly unnoticed. But sometimes I like ironing, as I used to like hanging up white voile dresses for five little girls to wear on Sunday morning. I can come back into the rumpled world wanting to be an iron directed by some hand not mine. I can have a new sense of the current even as I can feel outrageously satisfied that the wetted voile is thoroughly dried by that iron and miraculously stiff and pert for my having had a go at it. And that while it might last, my daughters, my dolls could be ready for anything. Most likely? A climb in the birch or skate around the hopscotch. Anything but a quiet seat in church. Like me, Mother, like me?

I hung her curtains on cleaned rods against windows washed with the ammonia she would have insisted on. For ten minutes I felt pristine, dauntless, yes, holy.

I laughed. "Mother, how do you like them? Really? So do I."

Heritage

This house is still half yours, Mother.

On close terms now with death, I live
in your quarters, among your mirrors
and closets, disclosed as you were
by how I muffle my agonies
and celebrate the sunlight.

If shutters make their geography
over the lace of your curtains,
I summon your naming of things
to fit the coming dark: Gumption.
Stick-to-itiveness. Heart.
Blessedness.
Coming to pass.

4

On Choices

The trouble is, the choices never get easier.

Shall I get to my studio early to begin a new chapter or plant the flat of primroses in the newly spaded garden by the aspen?

Shall I invite three grandsons to the cabin for a bonfire and overnight visit or have a quiet time there to black the stoves or finish that new book of essays by my friend?

Shall we have lunch for our weekly get-together, my daughters and I, or play tennis, or shop for summer tops, or maybe do all three while we talk?

Shall I take Liska, four, to buy the roller skates we didn't have time to get on her birthday spree, or take Aunt Edna to Ogden for a funeral?

Should I read the daily papers early rather than wait until midnight to do my job, or write notes to reporters who've written especially well this week?

Shall I call Chicago to talk about the progress of the memoir of my friend Clarice Short or check first with the university press here about publishing her poems?

Shall I do the final inputting of the murder mystery five of us just finished or hire someone to so that I can work on a column for *Exponent II* and try to finish revisions on *Russia?*

Shall I be extravagant and call a daughter or a friend long distance on daytime rates just because I feel like it, or be sensible and wait till our usual after-eleven call tonight?

Shall we plan to go to two wedding receptions tonight or the gala for Citizen of the Year that we've been sent tickets for? Or try to crowd in all three? Or none, and flit to a movie, or better still, call some friends to watch a video at home?

Shall I get my snow tires off and that lube that was to be at how many miles? or that Pap smear—how many times postponed?

And how is that friend doing with the bar exam coming up? And how did that other friend's talk go? And how are my old friend's shingles? And what were the results of that daughter's blood pressure check?

Could a friend and I work in a walk and have a workout as well as a visit? Or maybe just some very quiet time?

If I were smart, I'd get that lesson ready before the night before.

And how great would it be to tackle the storage room that still has Christmas paraphernalia strung from makeshift barber chair to costume trunk to hanging discards for Deseret Industries? And I could have laundry going while I did that.

And my brothers all want us to play golf together, a first in how many years? But it would have to be at the same time that I was going to a meeting. Maybe some rearranging?

And my once office-sharing friend from India will be gone before we have a visit if not today.

Oh, and that manuscript—I promised to have it read by tomorrow—right after erranding to the drug store, post office, optical shop, the vet for shots Pip should have had in February, Paul's birthday, the bank, the store—these days nobody to help unload and put away or to be pleased at what I bought.

Maybe take some treats to the kids later or take a bike ride with Mel at five?

And at midnight, can I stay awake to write in my journal while the day is still immediate? Or write that letter or read that story or talk over news or just plain say an intimate good night or wonder or pay attention to what slowing down can filter into my tiredest pores and prayers if I just let it . . .

Whoever suggested that life simplified itself, in or out of a house or family, as we go along? Whoever supposed that choices become one whit easier at over fifty or even sixty than at under thirty? And who would dare to suggest that keeping up with it all could ever be possible? Or, if impossible, manageable? The real trouble is that I *like* it all, want it all.

That I am in a different time seems to affect very little the difficulty in making the choices. Not a generality has changed, only the specifics. With the children married, the house "empty," I wrestle still with choosing to be alone to write and think or to be with those I want so much to be with. The only peace I can make with why I don't spend more time writing is that my real profession constantly calls me. It seems as important to live life as to record it. Trying to explain to someone not living in Mormondom, especially one who lives outside Salt Lake City, why I am unable to "call my time my own now that all my children are raised and gone" is like trying to explain the struggling of a salmon against the current in the season that calls. When asked "What do you do, Emma Lou?" all I can think to answer now is, "What I guess I've done but not recognized all along—I 'do' people. Most of us do."

And they "do" me. They fill and excite and inform and comfort me. Reciprocity is the name of any credible exchange. And that's what keeps bringing me back and back to the never-simplified complexity of living in the house that is mine, the house that draws me in and ushers me out fed, drained, certain, bewildered, but tuned in my soul to the blessings of being part of it all.

Some of what I've learned in passing, in choosing:
1. Every decade is easier—so far. Luckily we learn a lot in any ten years. Most days now, I get up thinking, Hey! Nothing hurts

and everything works! Wow! With my health—spiritual and mental as well as physical—I can take on any day with the equanimity of a racehorse, a little plump but groomed and trained for the track. And even when I do hurt—a stiff shoulder, a kinky back, a burny eye, a weary or saddened heart—another year or ten of learning how to heal—myself or others—has helped more than a twenty-year-old ever could imagine.

2. I must remember to pray at night, plan in the morning. Tired, I'm not good for much. The night, if entered in tune and expectant of answers, can provide what I never could. Somewhere between sleeping and waking is an informing that can furnish the day as no staying up and willing it so could do. If I trust it—the Muse, perhaps, or the higher sources of inspiration, the Light of Christ, the Holy Ghost—what is beyond my conscious command can lend reason and sometimes even calm to whatever needs me most.

3. Nothing is hard that has a visible end. Even labor pains when timed are endurable because a letup is in sight. The last lunge across the end of a day of closet cleaning is not as hard as the first, because at the end of the day the satisfaction outweighs the exhaustion. Even being up in the night with a sickness is muted if that sickness has a built-in cure time. When I'm dead center in any calamity, it is pacing to the end that can fill and save me.

4. A day—or a night—is not made up of hours but of segments. I cannot afford to forget the value of fifteen minutes. In that time, I can choose to clear the kitchen, or make three calls, or have a shower, or get a hug (some hug!), or read a whole paper's headlines or nine chapters in the book of John, or pick and make an arrangement of geraniums and Oregon grape—or close my eyes. What is eternal progression but the relishing of its particulars?

5. A relationship, even with someone I care most about, must be a gratuity, not an identity. It must be the same with my home as with a person. As soon as either becomes a means of identifying who I am, I have lost track of me. Within that relationship or that home, no matter how loving, I must maintain a clear sense of myself as an individual with choices that are mine as much as are my genes and upbringing. Only as that unique person can I walk not

leaning but shoulder to shoulder with my loves and with my happiest destiny in any home I get to occupy. By the same token, only as my fulfilled self can I maintain a pitcher full enough to pour from for anyone or any place that calls my name.

6. The best thing I have to offer anywhere is a happy person. Unhappy, I have nothing to give; I become part of the problem instead of part of the answer. Only by choosing from my own sources of good can I be a credible, let alone tender, woman of my home or anywhere else. Never can I be my best simply as part of the "preposition world": wife of, mother to, doer with. I must be more than secretary, chauffeur, chief cook and bottle washer, even manager over or lover of anybody.

7. To respect my own integrity is to cultivate the same in others. I do this by choosing and by then compartmentalizing, loving the moment even as it closes out what else might have been. As my friend Clarice Short said more than once to me, "Emma Lou, be firm or don't complain." It is not easy not to be greedy, not to wish for more than can ever be in any given period of time. Still, to be even minimally content, I must remember: The choices are, after all, ultimately up to me. And they don't all have to be made today.

8. Somewhere I have to have time just with me. Ann Morrow Lindbergh says: "If one sets aside time for a business appointment, a trip to the hairdresser, a social engagement, or a shopping expedition, that time is accepted as inviolable. But if one says: I cannot come because that is my hour to be alone, one is considered rude, egotistical, or strange. What a commentary on our civilization, when being alone is considered suspect; when one has to apologize for it, make excuses, hide the fact that one practices it — like a secret vice." (*Gift from the Sea* [New York: Vintage Books, 1977], page 50.) Secret vice or no, it must be practiced if I am to stay whole and able to be anything at all for anyone else.

9. What I must learn to be is myself. My heroes and heroines can light my way, my family and friends can inspire me, my sense of duty and loving-kindness can impel my willingness to take on the world. But only God and I can know who I am and what is the full measure of my creation. To that is my ultimate obligation, at

home more than anywhere else. My family will learn from my sense of myself and my world, and my responsibilities will be lighter for their being born of loving what I have to do.

10. I must start. Nothing is more immobilizing than indecision. And nothing is more discouraging than more to do than seems possible even to get at. Sometimes the only way I can handle even the pleasures of a busy day is to set them down, maybe on a list in the night—I have a trusty "pen light" nearby that allows me to jot almost in my sleep and not disturb a soul. Since sleeping is one of the things I do best, I want not even to disturb myself! And then, next day, I get to click them off *one at a time*. Satisfaction!

But it *is* critical to compartmentalize. I must let whatever choice is up have its way with the moment. And I must be thoroughly present for its serendipities, not waste energy or attention on what ifs. And then leave room, especially in my psyche, for spontaneity. Who knows what phone call or drop-in trade or idea might bring a lot more delight than interruption. There is, after all, always tomorrow.

We're great catch-up creatures. Once started, we can move through choices—especially quiet ones—nibbling and clearing, savoring some simply out of relief at their being done. After a vacation or even after sickness or surgery, it's possible to come back calmed, smelling the rain or violets and hearing our inner music in ways that our "normal" hectic pace seldom allows.

My tempo, my rhythms, my attentions, my faith are what I have to give. In the best of relationships, inside the homes I have occupied, they are what have been given me. While circumstance may alter any at any time, they are what can make what I do worthwhile. That they are given freely—and with wholehearted respect for my choices and for those I am lucky enough to live with —is what I owe to any homemaking at any stage. Only out of such choosing can any of us who live together become all that we were intended to be, as not only children of God but also as adults realizing both our divine and our human potential. So it's hard. Wasn't choice and the right to it what got us here in the first place?

And if my choices are seldom simple, so? At least I'm here and I get to make them.

Patience

Impossible to know,
but will there be more
or fewer exquisite choices
in the kingdom of light?

More or less exquisite anguish
in letting the different
weights of splendor or duty
fall in these steady rhythms
of sleeping and waking up?

Will patience and mortal
impatience balance the irregular
detail of what was a week?

Will lyrical arms gently lift
what glistens on the hook of a day
and draw like a magnet
beautiful and welcoming
what is behind the whole
to shimmer in casual
Wait and See?
Of course, says the editor
of wait and see.

5

On Being Saved from Domestic Tranquility

It had been one of those days—the whole day. Started off with the brakes going out on the car, grinding like gravel in an oil barrel. Blast! The whole morning gone with leaving my trusty Fiesta Plum to be fixed and me in the fix of no car. "So why not a day of sweet domesticity," I asked myself, "a catching-up time? Deep cleaning—really deep. C'mon, kid. Really deep!"

Start with the twenty-four-year-old heat vents in the floor of the playroom. Determination. Cement dust has plagued them for years. Cheesecloth covers can strain off some dust, but with winter coming, the furnace on, they should be cleaned. Definitely, they should be cleaned. Out with the tank vacuum, off with the brush, into the deep skinny rectangle with the hose.

Bam! The lid blows off the vacuum like Mount Saint Helens. A spume of grey. Fine silt settles on the piano, the rug, the couches, on the plants, the books. Wonderful!

Call the furnace-cleaning number on the furnace. No answer. Lunchtime. Warm some soup for lunch, a sure calmer-downer. Pour the soup into a bowl. The wooden handle on the blackened aluminum pan from the trousseau . . . turns. Whoosh, soup all over the shelf, my favorite Levi's, the lucky meant-to-take-spills old rubber-backed carpet, and—oh, no!—before time to daub it up, down the front of cabinets to dribble into four drawers! Swell!

Clean the cupboards off. Get into the drawers. The sugar bin needs filling. To the fruit room for the big twenty-pounder bought for economy. Start to pour while answering the phone. Don't notice a hole in the side of the sack. Too late, notice the mound of sugar on the floor. Scoop, sweep, break out the upright vacuum. Terrific!

Definitely enough deep cleaning. Turn on the dishwasher. Downstairs to desk. Fifteen minutes of mail, papers. Time to put a third wash in dryer. Open door to laundry room. Waterfall from ceiling. Somewhere up there—flood. Race back to kitchen afloat in two inches of steaming water. Dishwasher pumping out like the magician's mill. Great!

Two hours and twenty-eight minutes on cleanup. Hands blistered from wringing out towels. The back a fretful comma from cleaning up water, soup, sugar. Dandy!

So much for a day of domestic calm. Funny to look back on, actually not too funny while happening. Fortunately the exception, not the rule.

But enough to remind me that I like housekeeping best as a part-time thing. Naturally that's why I've spent great chunks of my thirty-seven married years trying to find how to make more less, and less more likable as I work at it less and less.

What in the world would my world have felt like on that day of domesticity if that house and its whims had been all there was?

Repair

The lights were out
all over
and the man who came

ran his green truck
into our
driveway because of

the pole. My T
V and stove,
washer, iron, and

lights were out and
I'd flipped all
the switches in the

box from on to
off and back
and nothing had hap-

pened. So when this
man arrived
with his starched name on

his green shirt I
was glad. In
fact when he climbed the

pole step by step
and dangled
there and fiddled with

things and the lights
came on I
said now there's a man!

6

On Balance

It was late in life to begin. I was forty-seven, had brought five daughters to adolescence, had welcomed a husband home to dinner every night without fail for twenty-two years, had for fifteen years shared our home with a mother who had rooms in a wing of our home where she did not need to be lonely in her aloneness of widowhood. For seventeen years I had loved having a preschooler. Our extended families included nearly forty on each side, all intriguing and close. I had friends I never got enough of, taught part-time at the university the English I never tired of, served for six years on the general board of the Young Women's Mutual Improvement Association of my Mormon church and worked with projects and people I was captivated by. Once in a while I even got to write.

But I was never alone. And I was busy dying.

My cup was running over and over, the saucer could not hold the overflow, and I was disappearing into the caffeine-free dregs.

The year I was thirty-nine I kept the only diary ever of every day, maybe in part to see if it was real, the pace, the demand, the bondage to what I loved. It must have been. There was only one small page per day, usually crowded and hardly readable, written I knew just before sleep. I never had either time or inclination to read back over those days until twenty years later. I dug it out and for three hundred miles, while he drove, I read it to Mel and we laughed. It all erupted full-color and life-size: A household of nine to maintain; five children under ten; often an unwed mother from social services—we loved and learned from them and they freed me to take on things like fifty chickens casseroled for a Relief Society dinner; three Little League tennis teams with daughters to coach; one freshman English class to teach three times a week on the run; papers to grade Sunday night while fixing a "smorgy board" and watching a movie on TV that made us all cry; boating trips with neighbors; conventions with Mel's business; being nearly forty before my first commercial air flight.

Six years after that diary, when our youngest started first grade full day, I started graduate school to get my master's degree in creative writing. Almost all of that writing would be done between 11:00 P.M. and 3:00 A.M. when everyone was in bed and it was quiet in my makeshift study among the storage shelves in the basement.

None of it I had to do; all of it was of my opting. I was a lucky woman and I knew it, prayed only "Help me to deserve."

But I was busy dying. And I didn't know why.

The following year I had back surgery, a fusion to repair an old skiing injury. I was away from everything for the first time in my married life, in the hospital for thirty-one days. I started a journal; again I didn't know why. On those pages in a wobbly hand there appeared, as if from invisible ink, explanations of why I was dying and reasons for finding ways not to, either physically on that high hospital bed of pain and turning grey, or emotionally in that wildly full home of love that I would be returning to.

I found what I needed and had never had—time to be alone. Even in that hospital, too medicated to read, too hurting to move, it was succulent to lie and think, not to have to be reporting in or doing anything anywhere. I must have hungered for it from the time I left my girlhood room at twenty-five to marry. There I had always had the chance to be by myself, being the only girl in a family of brothers. As much as I loved playing with those boys and being with my friends—close ones filling in for the sister I never had—every night I had time alone to let the day run through me, to read, to think, to dream, and always since I can remember, to write. And to be in touch with the power that I never doubted was there in prayers.

All of it was private, furnishing, letting me go to sleep riding moonbeams out the window to a sky that enveloped me for the night as soccer at recess, columns of figures and book lists in school, and jacks on the porch did in the day. Yes, I was a happy little girl, both sides of me—the active and the contemplative—legitimate and fed, approval for both as certain as my never even asking myself, Am I loved? or, Do I love? Like breathing out and in, the taking for happy granted the life of the body and the mind interacting with the life of the spirit.

Busyness and quiet. The balance.

It was not until I was forty-seven—eight years after that first diary—that I started from my hospital bed a life of journal keeping and found at last the reinstituting of that other life within me.

Between ages forty and forty-six, for nearly seven years of my life I had spent Wednesdays, all day and often far into the night, with the YWMIA, chairing a committee rewriting manuals, serving on another committee planning June conference. Included too, of course, were maybe thirty hours a week trying to get ready for Wednesdays.

My family had been as great as could realistically be expected. It was Mother off to do her Church work, Dad theoretically home to support everybody in whatever might come up on Mother's Wednesday night at the board, which often meant him on the phone with business and girls on their own with anything but. "A wholesome growth for everyone" was the consensus outside our home; inside was often up for grabs.

But support was there, in spirit. For all the years of our married life, any Church job that had needed me had had me, and the support had been willing from Mel, involuntary from the girls. If it hadn't always come with ease, it always came with love.

During those thirty-one days in the hospital, which meant a release at my request from the general board, I thought, Why not a board night for the rest of my life? Only now, one reserved for my own agenda? Still for Mel and the girls a chance to find their hectic ways to each other with me out of the way? Still for me a breather from being central to every day and night in a household of eight?

So we talked it over, and mostly happily ever after, Wednesday was sacrosanct, Mother's day and night away. I was to take it as a time to do whatever struck my fancy—in the same way that Mel went to a movie to relax after teaching real estate for three hours on Thursday nights.

A whole lot did strike my fancy—a frolic on the ski hill or especially on the tennis courts. Dinner with a friend or relative also usually caught in the grind. A play, a movie, time in the library to roam stacks or sit in a carrel and read or write. Time to drive with an aunt to Ogden to see fall come. A night adrift at the cabin, a book rescued from the pile of "read this immediately." A trip to Provo to see a new baby. Mostly and always, time to think, to be in touch with the world that spun somewhere outside the home where I most of the time loved being. Sometimes I worked, sometimes I played, sometimes with others, sometimes alone. Always I came back fully feathered with "OK, everyone, Mama's home— really home—and feeling terrific!"

In the seventeen years since the surgery that fixed my back and gave me a new life, I have happily indulged the mending of other sections of me by my Wednesdays away. Of late, I even have a studio seven minutes but eons from home. No phone, no contact, no obligation—simply a place to play at my word processor and leave everything stacked and scattered with no hand or eye but mine to see or disturb.

Along the years, Wednesdays have not always been the most convenient time to leave. I have missed dinners out, PTA gatherings, crises, hilarities. I have returned to disasters, discords, even a message that "Elaine has been trying all night to get you, Mother. You were supposed to speak to hundreds of people somewhere."

Of course it has not always been with great cheer or cheers that I have left my household. But I knew from the beginning that those Wednesdays would be respected only if I respected them, that in addition to being anxiously engaged in good causes I had to believe that it was right that I should be engaged as well in my own cause.

At first, it was hard. Sometimes I hated leaving even as I loved it. Always there was the reality that nothing comes without a price. It took about as much courage as anything I'd ever done to just do it. Not to have to justify or make everything OK for everyone else before it was OK for me. Goodness knows, I'd been trained that way. Even on the general board we had our little helpful printed tips on how to make even our being away on assignment—no easy assignment, ever—not an imposition on those we left behind, grown-up or otherwise. After all, who else in a family could be cheerleader and provider of the household that was as much theirs as the woman's?

But then the family began planning around those Wednesdays as they had around my board nights. They fixed their own meals or went out for a hamburger together. They depended on each other for help with homework, solace in trauma, fun in being a family. For Mel it was a chance to get beyond the how-did-the-day-go? with his five daughters, and for them it was a rich opportunity to know their dad, who was gone many more nights than one a week for business, teaching real estate, bishoping as spiritual leader to three hundred single students in a university ward. Over most of our daughters' lives, Mel was a whistling, jovial ghost occupying now and then a seat at the table or the organ or along the row in church or in the big black leather chair, reading or watching the news—someone to hug hard, get multiple kisses from, go on vacation with, and watch going out of the door early and late, sleeping whenever he could because the day had stripped him even as it had layered our lives with what was good and essential.

When I came back from my time away, Mel and the girls had struggled and become something of a unit they might never have been with me there; and I was welcomed as I might never have been had I not been not there. I became someone with a life like theirs, full of things away from home and them that interested and compelled and altered me just as theirs did them. And what a time we had sharing what had propelled us all in different directions.

Because we had always played as well as worked together, even when they were still young, my children knew me as more than a series of functions. So did Mel. But now, with our Wednesdays, Mel welcomed me in new ways as more than the mother of his children and the keeper of his home—and with new respect for that too, having spent one night in seven in full charge of the domain. I now wish I could have reciprocated more in his awesome daily burden of making a living that allowed all the living that he provided for us. I did do some of that by learning to do better what I did outside our home and sometimes to get paid for it—another happy by-product of that time away.

These days I see our daughters establishing patterns of intermittency with husbands and family, roommates, jobs, pressures— making a space in which to let talents out and steam off safely. I hope the results will matter as much for them and their households as they have for me and ours.

Not everyone needs the time alone that I do. Mel grew up sharing a bedroom with a brother, men in the army, students in a dorm. Being alone was not at first a comfortable thing to him, never probably will be what it is to me. But for most women, I would suspect, it is vital to have time to be unaccountable, time for reflection as well as for action. Claiming time to be alone could be the difference between dying from the inside out and being very much alive everywhere.

When I asked a group the question, "What is your favorite sound?" a mother of six children said, "The hum of the refrigerator." And every young mother laughed—but nodded. Quiet just might be the scarcest and most valuable commodity in most households that include children—or a TV.

In the past ten years I have learned about going really away— out of town to artist retreats, workshops, symposia, where others are working with the same intent and joy, or to quiet places where I can have time all to myself to occupy that mystic realm of creative insistence. In either, I thrive. But no matter how satisfying the time away, I am invariably ready or willing to come back, mended, fed, stronger, and richer, to take on my life that is still not so dif-

ferent from what was recorded in those pages of a diary nearly
twenty-five years ago.

The Other Face of the Moon

There is a place for the undark solitude
away from growing into and going under.
You must emerge like the moon from clouds.
You must learn from the tides.

What you remember most of that life before
was a you running breakneck into
breakfastlunchdinner, wrapped and packaged:
in Little Leagues, rolls, programs,

the well-being of casseroles and showers:
a you honed by lists and hand-to-hand
combat with schedules, all with overwhelming
accompaniment room-to-room wall-to-wall.

Despite how you cared for the others
you could have been an alarming
picture against the unending landscape
of feeding and voices, causes, celebrations,

crises, deadlines, and bedtimes. And
Loveliness. Loving. Play. Even the cabin
a slide in the deluge. But something
drew you back, gave warning:

Everything wavers; even the protected
must escape their protectors. What was
waiting to be let out was you. The you
willing to notice, with the audacity to choose.

II

Before you were married, your mother's
fold-out desk in your own room in that house
of brothers washed you into bed with what
came from a day, a page, ideas riding the moon

to make themselves at home. On the best dreamers
nothing is wasted. Half a lifetime later,
beginning to see, you stirred deliciously, knew
that formulas, pharmacies, or dictums could not

have helped you. Only prayers and not waiting longer
for the unclouded moon seen only in Stillness:
That being between what was listed, separate
from even the kisses savory from mouth to mouth.

You would leave indefinite in all but the leaving,
hostile to nothing. In some room of your own
you would pass time with no one waiting for you,
exquisitely slow, no problem with

the business of eating or answering calls.
Sleep would inform you and morning would be wise.
You would find what was there: the other face
of the moon and Stillness.

III

Everything gathered that first time:
Away, crisp, solitary, deliciously anonymous,
you flew onto paper, slept through ablutions,

skipped meals, gorged on drifting, a walk,
a bath, a book, going to the end of a thought,
being surprised by Light, listening listening.

But away was not by itself enough either.
Day after day even of stillness told when
it was time you reentered, came face to face

with the intimate detail of fingers and sentences
mixing with yours. Passion started up
for a place not empty of misfortunes, for doorbells

and phones, pot roast and broccoli, you deployed
plate by plate, lucky to be called by voices
to the luringest colors of fire, the sweet-smelling uproar,

the eyes, the skin soliciting, warm,
the moon hidden in the landscape,
you inebriate of their offerings.

IV

As in the moon's cycle of phases
there are stretches that befit the season.
For thirty-one married years
you thought by giving what you had

to the one life you assumed you had chosen,
all would be repaid in the currency
of your own blood, voice, approval of elders,
the fancies of small children.

After all, didn't your family explain you?
The others reward in kind? But your obligation
was to sing in yourself as well as to those who called
for your song. No one loves anything always the same.

If the gift of quiescence is denied even the joyous lover,
the spirit contorts in its own unwinding.
Finding your way away you did no harm except perhaps
to the death of that spirit. Whatever you took

from either life you raised up in the other
alongside spines stronger, shining cheeks not ever
forgotten, flourishings in your departures, sure
of your hungering to return. You alive and paying

attention. Your pages wait to be finished,
may never be. But Stillness plays on the other face
of the moon and you, restive and calm, hang tough
between phases, knowing when to let it be.

7

On Quality Time

I grew up mothering with Mary Ellen Chase's conviction that "I love you with all my heart, but not with all my time." I thought that quality could make up for quantity when I had so many compulsions propelling me both at home and out of the door. I was wrong, of course. Nothing ultimately can make up for time with a loved one, especially a mother. There are times when only a mother can be enough.

It was not until she was married herself that one daughter confessed, "Oh, Mom, when I was sick I didn't want anyone but you —and it's still the same." In those days, so often frantic to be enough, I was writing poems like "Rip Off":

> Call me mother! Call me daughter!
> Call me wife! Call me friend!
> Rip off splinter. Here . . .
> as the pulling at the scrawny frays
> twirls me shredded
> in the tactless wind of waning . . .
> untouchable
> between the devouring breaths

of time and circumstance
and wanting to be
enough.

So impossible to be enough. So easy to fall into the trap of asking, like Golda Meir, even now—after any effort or joy—"Who or
what have I neglected today?"

At the same time, I was always grateful that they wanted me
around, glad that our times together were so rich as to be
"morish," as my father would say about Mother's chocolate cake
—for all of us. To get more precious time together, I took my children one at a time on general board trips with me, and our weeks
at the cabin were exclusively ours, not interrupted by anything.
But of course our times at home were what made up our lives. And
they were often busy maintaining—preparing meals, clearing up,
keeping the chaos minimal as we visited about whatever was there.
For all of its demands and often frustrations and griefs, somehow I
always felt mothering was my forte. Because almost always it was,
continues to be, my love.

I too always wanted more. But I cannot go back. Neither can I
make up for deficiencies in the past by wishing or guilt in the present. And I likely would have done not much differently if I could.
We do what we can, we are what we are. To expect more of ourselves is to be mired in discouragement if not despair, the most un-
productive of sentences for anyone. We're all basically paddling to
stay afloat the best way we know how. With no two of us ever mus-
tering in the same way, how we do it is more to be understood
than criticized.

Not that I need always hide my troubles or camouflage my
wars with them. But I must find ways not to wallow in inertia or
give in to *velleity*—a wonderful word a Catholic friend in Tulsa
gave me—"a mere wish that does not lead to the slightest action."
Ultimately the thing I really have to give is a happy person, not as
a mood but as a mode, to make me someone eligible for someone
else's wanting to be with—or hear from. That I have to figure out
and allow responsibly as only I can.

I have a ninety-five-year-old friend, Margaret Torkelson,
whose house is a delight to visit because her wars with crumbling

bones and inadequate energy and even pain never deplete her sense of humor and proportion. No Pollyanna, still she is never the prophet of gloom that age and loneliness sometimes create in the most expectant of us. She waves me off smiling and wanting to return. "Don't forget to notice my roses, dear. They're lovelier than ever this year." Of course I return and return—to hear her say, "I love you lots of much."

As with Margaret, much of what we have to give each other, though, demands time apart from other time—a hard thing to come by most days and in most households. In our adult years, my children and I could do a lot of passing in the dark of communal get-togethers—the big family dinners, holidays, family outings— all bubbling with exchange and overflowing with personnel. Even daily calls with those in the same city or semiweekly with those away can be only so deep. The "one-on-ones" (how I hate that overworked catchphrase) are what sustain us.

Every week for years we've gone to lunch on Thursdays, any daughters in town and I. We plan around it, schedule to go to a different place every time. They get baby-sitters, I put off appointments, we all keep it sacrosanct. Table talk there is different, candid, often frivolous, sometimes sad, never surface. We talk of ideas, plans, griefs, excitements. We stay in touch.

On their birthdays, I get to take each grandchild on a spree. Alone. We go to the cabin and stay overnight, or we go out to dinner somewhere new. We shop for a precious item, find the unusual, the un-thought-of—or the much thought about. Once James celebrated his tenth April birthday with me at the end of my month's stay alone writing in a friend's empty condominium in Sun Valley. He helped me name the book just finished, we rode horses and swam, the two of us the only ones in a pool steaming in a snowstorm. We had the best nachos in town in a place where he could play pinball; and we drove home with him naming Transformers for a grandma to whom that word meant relays on top of telephone poles. Last year Nicky, his Beatles tapes, and I celebrated his fourteenth birthday in the same fashion, and this year Grace came for her tenth, loving the games on my computer almost as much as she loved riding a horse.

Out of the crowd, I get to know each as a person apart—and

they get to know me as something more than Grandma Grey, regardless of how much fun we have at the cabin or in the dictionary
at home.

My favorite time with my sons-in-law is when they drop by for
a chat or to make a phone call or when we get to play together.
Three of them who didn't play tennis until marrying our tennis-
wild girls have been out to get me on the court in blood battles
that we laugh and sweat over, me telling them as I have my daughters that when they beat me it will be the happiest and the saddest
day of my life. On the other hand, the other two of them are professional tennis players, and with winning ways they hit with me,
grinning me into believing I might be ready next year for anything
—Wimbledon maybe? At Thanksgiving this year in Carmel, California, where one family invited us—not bad, Thanksgiving at
someone else's house—I got to play golf with three of "my boys,"
one playing as my partner whose best ball won us the champion-
ship. Of what? Nobody knew or cared.

But even that fun does not compare with what happens when
we talk alone, often when we're working on a project at their
homes or ours, especially at the cabin. We talk about a plan for set-
ting up a business, about meditating and blessings, about building
a new arm in surgery, about finishing a Ph.D., about a new way to
teach a forehand. As a group of five, they are the tall husbands my
daughters love, never dull, invariably good-hearted good men.
Alone, they are the sons I never had, the blessing in our later lives
that balances whatever satisfactions we had before they came
along.

And once a year, my five daughters and I have a "girls' trip,"
without husbands or children—four or five days, preferably on nobody's home turf. The first year it was at the tennis camp in Ojai,
California, that our fourth daughter, Dinny, and her husband,
Mike, ran in the summer. We slept in the infirmary, ate in the cafe-
teria, lolled by the pools, played on the courts, and hiked in the
hills. We talked, we were silent. Everything was easy. On a beach
in nearby Santa Barbara, after mostly window shopping, we even
bore testimony to each other of the divine at work in our lives—a
rare opportunity for intimate connection.

These times away from the keeping of a house or anything else except our meaning to each other are a rare and delectable part of keeping a home. We go back to our households refurbished with each other, partners in creating better times, better lives for ourselves and for those we live with. It never fails. We come home fed, ready to feed.

Now that three out of five of the families live away, our cozy time together is more vital than ever. I realize that when they were all at home it was simple to tell one story, have one work party or ski trip, and include all. Now it takes five times as much to clarify or inform or say I love you to each one—plus their broods. If time was hard to come by and give in the old days, it's even harder now—and maybe more important. As adults we need each other as the launching that being part of a home can provide. Not to be leaning or dependent, but to be operating in our separate circles with the equanimity furnished by knowing we are loved.

For my husband and me, now it can be much the same. Our oldest son-in-law has taken over Mel's real estate business—his lifelong "housekeeping"—and now has all the worries even as Mel has the privilege of being in transition. Still, he has his own desk there, can come and go, work or not work, be consultant and senior professional even as he takes more time for lunch or a trip or for our riding the two new bright red mountain bikes he came home with to surprise me only last week.

Quality time is hard to come by. To pretend I have more hours or energy than I do is to fracture myself and those to whom I can offer sometimes less than any of us would like. The best I can do is try, now in ways I never could with the house overflowing. One at a time. Always wanting more. The struggle not very different from what it was ten, twenty years ago. But worth it. Any time.

Going to Bed Alone and Far Away

What I'm afraid is
that midnight will arrive

before morning, splendid,
and I will be asleep.

And maybe—this could happen—
that the children of my children
will grow up before me
and go charging off past
where I can tell them a story
and touch off their birthdays.

And that I will forget how love
carries on with aspens shaking their
thousand brown curls at April

and with the intimacies of
syllables and octaves
and that I will be where return
is not part of the plan.

8

On the Emptying Nest

One day they simply are gone. The house they filled is part of their history, the homes they establish then the making of history, as are their departures.

A typical day of such ending and beginning was the Sunday before Rinda and Jim's wedding, now nearly fifteen years ago. Becky had married Paul that same year, and was expecting her first baby. Dinny would soon be off for a semester of study in England, and Megan in not too many years would be an AFS student in Haddonfield, New Jersey. In only another two years, Shelley would be next to marry. And even as their departures were everything we could have hoped for, each time it was hard.

Hold

Only one more Sunday and she'll be gone.
But now she plays her violin, old songs
That drew her from the squawking bow to trembling
Sweetness that singes these last frayed, jumbled
Days with aching for suspension. Not return.

No not even to the pulling, blurting
Years of simple acquiescence to demand—
The changing, feeding, cleaning, running strands
Laid upon each other, patterning
This closeness into womanhood, flattening
Our prints into this time of hard goodbye.
Unbreathed. Just holding. To suffocate the sigh
That will wisp her off to some strange place for
Drawing music from new, harsh strings and score.

Surely for good, but gone. Each time the going, going, gone would be done by another of those pals who had often come in from waitressing at Marie Callender's at midnight to say, "Mother, let's go to the cabin!" We would. I'd crawl out of bed sometimes to fly on the snowmobiles into the glistening cold, to build a fire or not in the big black stove, just to wake up in the fairyland where those girls had made quilts and read books and hiked to Castle Crags and swung on the big swing and made canyon toast in the Monarch stove with the tall chimney. Because Rinda's was a February wedding, she was the only daughter not to be able to choose the cabin for her reception, but she wore my wedding dress that would also fit the other three to follow despite their different sizes.

Now she was off on her new life. A huge change, the end of one phase for both of us, certainly the start of another. With me wanting, as I had with Becky and would with the others, to cling to the day before. Of course I rejoiced in her new happiness, the far more than adequate, the unbelievably able and aimed Jim, who would father her children and foster her celebrations of their life and hers, as Paul had for Becky.

Shelley was next to go. "After the Wedding", a poem about her, ended:

> And in this cool place of wilting names
> and baby's breath
> I am putting her slip
> into the laundry bag

and eating white frosted cake
as I vacuum up the blanks
and wonder where they go.

Suppose those blanks had been all I had to occupy me? How different would have been the filling of them. No matter how Nicky, Richard, and Michael, James, Katie, and Liska, Grace, Coulson, and Eric fill blanks, and baby Sammy assures us of life beyond life, since Dinny and Megan have married and gone our household is down to two. Dinny now has Mike plus Brittany and Warner, and Megan and Ed have brought us Daniel, our "Danny Boy" incarnate. But wondrous as the filling is, about none of it did I really have anything to say except, Be happy. And then only to be recipient of the changes that each of those years and each family member's fancies and fortunes have brought.

Our house is by most definitions now an "empty nest." Different. But not so different. Through it all, the keeping of that house, that home has mattered, has continued to be not everything, but a saving grace.

For instance five years ago our fifth daughter, Megan, was married at age twenty. Two years later she was divorced. It was an everything-perfect-married-to-a-returned-missionary-in-the-temple-gone-awry disaster, full of pain but luckily never bitterness. And no children. Only terrible sadness. A new kind of sadness for all of us to learn from.

She had set up a home with great expectations, moved it later into the basement of our empty nest with a great sense of failure. A tragic dynamic, again full of shifts to absorb—for all of us. I recognized again: You're about as happy as your least happy child. And again that the restorations come slowly and, even with faith, in a jagged course.

This was her poem of that time:

The Ruin

The basement is black
but in the noon hours the sun

streaks in so you can see.
It's like coming upon a pile of bones.
The chairs are tipped on top of their table
having dumped their occupants for dinner.
The forks are rolled in plastic
having touched too many lips.
The blanket has been pulled from under
the weight of those that were there
and in its fold is the smell of you.
The cord is wrapped around the buttons of the phone
hiding its face from my bulging eyes.
I know I cannot call.

It's like finding one of those ruins at Lake Powell
where all life has been blown away.
Only this time I am the dead
in this windless decimation.
My stomach is hollow
and in the box of pictures
all those teeth that show
belong to skeletons.

                    —Megan Thayne, 1983

So, having to put her household away in ours, how did house-keeping provide for either of us? Loved as she knew she was but had lost track of, she had to set about finding a new home—within herself first. And has. It took three years of urgent making-do. Of moving her household of one to Portland for a master's degree in social work. Of letting her housekeeping be not only in reclaiming her sense of worth through accomplishment, but in finding ways to let her "decimation" lend understanding and help to others. She had to housekeep in a basement apartment so dim that only her knack for arranging a plant and bookcase could let in light.

More important, in the dim she had to learn to let a Higher Power guide her, to trust in God, indeed to do as Mother always said, "Pray at night and plan in the morning." It took not even months but years to feel carefree again, to giggle, to open a day with faith in its coming to be. The most prized item of the time—a new used vacuum to bring her red and black shag and her spirits out of smashed dishevelment.

Last year she married again and is, still with smiling disbelief, putting a new home—a little house—and a career together with a wonder of a gentle, alive man who does cross-stitch with as much aplomb as he hits a ball or finishes his Ph.D. in exercise physiology, who is as openly thrilled as she is to hold and tend their new baby. A second chance the miracle, so full of joy for all of us, so much more carefully regarded even than a first.

Hers was one of how many agonies?—sickness, accidents, losses, fears—that are part of a household. Of loving the people in it. As a wise friend said to my mother when my father died suddenly at age fifty-nine, "If you'd loved him less, you'd miss him less. Would you trade?"

Who would? Mother's pain, Megan's pain was mine, was all of ours. As have been the trials of the rest of us. Yet we have to get through our tragedies. And for me, ministering to a household has invariably helped. In all of it, the crises as well as the hurts, adjustments to change have sent me sometimes reeling to housework for repair, no different now than in this poem of nearly twenty years ago:

Knowing That Most Things Break

You fondle routine's
tattered strings
hugging dailiness

blown
from room
to room

by dusty
urgencies

bent
against

remembering.

Patience. The hardest thing of all for me. I want the cure now. Housekeeping helps. Often it's possible to know the condition of my psyche and spirit by the shine on the house and whether my ironing is done. If it's too "done," it's a not good time. Mostly I like to keep house as I keep my desk—clear enough to see some glass, knowing that the projects it provides will rescue even as they compel and occupy me. With love as well as with insistence, yes even sometimes with desperation.

The spirit of personal housekeeping allows me to create a life not full of endings but of beginnings. I understand by now that even the lovely phases I like to call states of grace—when everyone is well and happy—will come and will go. As will the occupancy of my house and days. What will hold is the faith that says, Mother (named Grace), Father, you have bequeathed me far more even than the need for a tidy, livable, lived-in space. Your ordering is of my own wherewithal—to ask not for a change of circumstances but, with heaven's help, for a sense of worth in them and in me.

And the grace of your kind of gumption to take on what is there.

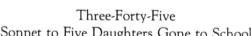

Three-Forty-Five
Sonnet to Five Daughters Gone to School
1965

Fly open, door, and let the chaos in!
Sweet silence, though delicious, now is stale.
The house, too neat, and in its order pale,
Resounds with lonely petulance. Begin
My life. Flood home, five girls, with brushed embrace,
With lengthy resumé of great events,
With wistful lot of unreserved laments.
Fly open, door, to a girlhood's breathy pace.
How far the day before that door will close

On brides no longer bent on quick return,
Whose lives will stretch beyond this childhood womb?
My loves, throw wide the door, your zests impose,
Immortalize your bubbling, brief sojourn
With nearness ringing loud in every room.

The Coming of Quiet
To a Home with Five Daughters Gone
1987

I could have declared, would likely believe
No day would come when the house all quiet
Would suit my heart, that I would not grieve
For the crowded rooms, the noisy diet.
Admittedly, eloquence sometimes came
One voice at a time, and silence crept
Light as a bird, the first to proclaim
The growing up and out as we slept.
But now this passage to silence and spaces
Throws up its hands, says, Make up your mind,
Choose: the clutch of voices, fingers, and faces?
Or unoccupied order? Strangely I find
This moment, that, that moment, this,
Each transient and lingering as a kiss.

9

On Learning by Being There

Things happen. They simply happen. In a home or away from home. Dealing with what happens is most crucial to being part of that home. To ask why? or why them? or why me? can be the least productive of concentrations. Why not me? Why not any of us? would seem more reasonable. And more efficacious. The unpredictable in life is often the best teacher, the saving grace of flexibility, the thing learned. And faith to pray not so much for "Please, with your omnipotence change all this," as for "Please, with your strength help me to manage."

It is not easy to learn, like Job, that kind of asking, but it can be a gift given—if I take time and am willing to wait for the teachings that accompany everything that happens in a day—or night. For instance:

Things happen. One night eight hundred miles away your third daughter, Shelley, calls, is filling with fluid, a complication in the last three months of her pregnancy. An ultrasound reveals fluid in the baby's head, abdomen, extremities. Hydrops. A fifty-fifty chance for survival; if born alive, a 25 percent chance of being without "multiple anomalies."

Scary. Both mother and child. Their other children were easy. Grace, almost eight, Coulson, four, Eric, two, need what they're used to having—loving attendance from their mother, in bed now, immobilized by dehydration from keeping nothing down for three days. You've longed to go, been told by Shelley to wait, they're OK, come when the baby comes—as planned for seven months with great excitement. Then Grace is on the phone when you call: "Oh, Grey, we need you. My mommy is so sick."

In three hours you're on a flight. For thirteen days you shift into automatic. You know how. Thirty-five years your apprenticeship; you're expert. The chaos that is a house without a mother is hastily brought to order. Pick up, smooth out, expose to soap and water. Same for children. Plus put in supplies, put out meals, slick up after. Works for the husband too, freed now to see his ailing Shelley in and out of hospital IVs and morphine.

Emotion in way past automatic, all the old tenderness, tediousness—the momentary triumphs of dealing with the immediacy and omnipresence of children, the redundancy of dailiness, the weary euphoria of bathing, playing, watching them learn, do, and undo, patting, reading them to sleep four, five times. With it, the old mama's concern for her own—Please let Shelley be OK. Camaraderie with "P" as he installs a new toilet in the half-finished bathroom for her, busyness his outlet too for waiting and anxiety. And like a refrain always just below the surface, Please let Shelley be OK.

Days pass like clouds moving across a broad sky. You lapse into familiarity with small hands, insistent routines, nights never uninterrupted, but sleep rewarding as it is only to the physically spent. Mornings, you're up and one-directional, unfragmented even as you spray out—into projects on the kitchen table, a tree house in the backyard; you buy a soft leather football to throw, tablets to draw on, Bingo for after dinner.

You drive the hour across the bay to San Francisco with Shelley, persistently expectant, for a sophisticated echocardiogram. You see the baby's heart, a throbbing finger's inch, declared robust. On the familiar, festive wharf, you have a tiny lunch—that Shelley loses just before you both laugh taking pictures of how huge she is. You get to visit alone with your skier, artist, believing mountain girl more than in the two years since the family left Salt Lake.

When she is braced and pillowed to never-easy-or-long sleep, "P" tells you over your late bowl of shredded wheat that he likes the name of Sam for the baby, asks what you think are his chances of living, and, if none, should they bury him back home?

This is new, not part of any automatic. You talk a lot with the Lord, say you know why he gave you your five when you were young, why you're glad you're still around to be in on this learning when you're not so young.

More tests, more complications. Amniocentesis, two quarts of fluid drained from Shelley's discomfort, only to be replaced in hours. You see Sammy's heart pulsing as you saw it on the screen as you swab up spills and gallop your fingers in shampooed hair on little heads laughing. You imagine another face to wipe spaghetti from and to kiss cuddled between you and a tyrannosaurus rex watching "Pinwheel" over Coulson's lunch. Grace shows you how the baby looks on page 89 of *The Miracle of Life*. That rapid baby-beat is what you sleep by. Shelley says she does the same, except she lies awake to wait for one more kick before she drops off, has "P" feel it too.

It is the day before her thirty-second birthday, the twenty-fourth of March. The all-girls' get-together with her four sisters, planned since last year, arrives. They all spend the days between her house and Dinny's in Carmel, two hours away, try to make everything normal. For four days, between emergencies and keeping house, you all laugh at *Beach Blanket Babylon* in San Francisco after linguini at the Italian Place, watch Katharine Hepburn and Nick Nolte in *Grace Quigley* on video, laugh, eat Chinese food into the night. Shelley does everything, ignoring her side taped to anchor a rib displaced by coughing combined with the horrifying distention. You all want to siphon off the pain, see Shelley radiant again. You talk as you always have, go to sleep counting off the miracles of the ten children of those daughters, marveling at the billion rightnesses that let them be.

Mel calls from home. A business crisis. You will fly home with Becky on one of your senior citizen passes, meet with him and clients. Here, another amniocentesis. Please, some relief. Also chromosome test results. You don't want to leave. Dinny and Megan will clean the house before they go back to their homes, the girls' trip over.

Eighteen hours later you are back, a part of what has now become like something scripted, not real. Rinda, who has stayed to cover, had called at 9:00 A.M. to say, "Shell's in labor." Only an hour before, Shelley on the phone saying all had died down, no rush.

At 1:20 from the Oakland airport you call labor and delivery. She has delivered, the baby is in intensive care. You ask, Is she all right? Yes. The baby, is he alive? Yes. Is he all right? You'll have to ask the father.

You hail a cab, say, Kaiser Hospital, hurry. The man with no English takes the slowest route through town, a thousand lights, eternity to the east entrance. You ask directions on the run, exit the elevator on 4, hunt down Recovery. Behind a white circle of curtain, arms open, Shelley and "P" say from the high bed, Sammy's heart is strong, his body is whole, a perinatal team of six are working on him in the ICU. Rinda says in private the delivery was a nightmare.

Now Shelley, safe—thank all that's holy—saying Sammy would make it, less fluid in him than they thought, that heart so strong. "P" out, gone to watch the team at work. You wait. Five minutes. Six. He is back, weeping. They've given up. The baby's dead.

You and Rinda leave them holding each other. In the hall the team, two crying. What was it? They couldn't get him to breathe. Forty-five minutes his life. Two doctors, a woman and a man, ask if the parents would like to hold their son. Behind the white curtain you gather, Rinda, the doctors, and you. Under a white bonnet Sammy's hair is black, curly over the blue scalp, forehead. His face is like Eric's, "Gerber" round, his lips parted for sucking. Shelley holds him with ancient adroitness, touching away his white blanket for all of you to feel his fingers, toes. Warm. "They look like mine, like Gracie's," says "P." You feast on him, his downy shoulders, ears, nose snubbed like Coulson's.

And then it's time. "P" picks him up, knows how, holds him close. Tears try to fill the emptiness when the doctors patiently lift him away, give Shelley the Polaroid pictures, three, taken when he was moving on his own. "His heart was so strong," says Shelley. "Couldn't it be given to another baby?"

Automatic you are not. Automaton you can become. Shelley and "P" need to be for each other. They will hold, not be apart now. You drive staunch, broken Rinda to the airport, drive the leviathan van back through 6:00 P.M. traffic, pay the baby-sitter, repair the house, spruce up the three to take back to the hospital to be told there, by the bed with their mother so they won't think anything has happened to her too, that Sammy is not coming home.

Sober and silent they listen, Eric clinging to you now, Coulson holding his dad's face between his four-year-old hands feeling his tears, Grace saying to her mother, "But I never got to see him alive," crying. The father and mother hold each one in new ways, washed with weariness.

You take the three across the street for burgers with "P" at a place where he has lunch most days with his friends on the physical therapy staff, then wave him back to Shelley. In the van on the freeway, all three fall asleep. Impossible for you to carry out and up and into bed, they stumble anywhere you lead, limp, holding tight, you too, to where home is.

Mortuary arrangements. How to get Sammy to Salt Lake for a burial plot owned by his other grandparents. A small obituary, plans for friends to call. Autopsy results reported by the almost glowing perinatal specialist: not genetic, not anything treatable, from the second month on, the diaphragm incomplete, chest cavity filled with digestive tract, lungs crowded out. No wonder he couldn't breathe.

You bring Coulson to Salt Lake early on his first plane ride, his favorite thing the blue water swirling in the steel toilet up there in the sky.

Two days, then the rest landing in Salt Lake, choices made, you seeing at the church the blue casket the size of a jewel box, inside it the unpuffy head and inch-long hands that you remembered warm and pliant. Grace saying, "He looks like a doll," stroking his hand. Coulson asking, "Is he fake now?"—the makeup heavy to hide the blue head. Eric, bewildered, pressing from one relative to another, big-eyed, solemn. Every friend they had wanted to be able to see, there, one saying an acacia tree would be planted for Sammy in the desert of Kenya.

"P" talking at the graveside in the bright sun. Born on his mother's birthday, Samuel Thayne Rich would continue, never not be part of what the family is. Five Rich sisters singing family songs with guitar. Rinda telling of Shelley and "P," the miracle makers, the expecters. Brahms' lullaby sung a cappella by a sister-in-law JoAnn on a blue-sky day right under Mount Olympus. The dedication of the grave by a brother, Jim. A holy day, a holy place.

That is all. "P" carrying two boys at once, Shelley in "civilians," her smile almost back, walking beside them as natural as on a stroll along their beach. Grace up ahead with cousin Katie, also seven, holding hands.

You ride to a late lunch at the church, a passenger along with grandsons twelve, ten, and nine years old, your husband grieving for needing to eat fast and be back to an appointment. The familiar washes across the day, the dear hearts and gentle people of your Relief Society feeding the crowd.

On the Saturday they have to stay over to get the rate on the airline, you hike the snowy road to the cabin with Coulson and "P." For Coulson you dig a stale Oreo out of the cookie jar, inspect the old tub full of last year's flies, blow the bugle to say, We're here. Standing beside "P," both of you searching the pines, the grey oak, the crags, the March silence expecting birds and green, you say to "P," "He's here. Sammy." "Yep," he says.

To the plane on Sunday with surprise bags from their other grandmother to open after takeoff. Waiting for boarding, you walk the boys around the airport, chubby fingers noticing the antique airplanes above the escalators. You talk hopscotch with Grace as you hug, say that in the summer you could draw another on the driveway and maybe graduate past ten. "P" squeezes you hard, and Shelley lets her tears out when you do. A sweetness stays like when she was born, that Sunday child. Then they are gone.

It is a long walk back to the car with Mel. A quiet one. Neither of you dares talk. And you are suddenly very tired, reminding yourself: Nothing is hard that has a visible end.

Things happen.

You go home to the blessedness of routine, of others to love. But not the same. More. Then you will look toward April, away, writing maybe, exploring what happened, back to normal, whatever that is. With Sammy's heart going right along.

Sammy Asleep
For the Baby Who Lived an Hour

This is more than an angel cradled
in the blue husk
of what has been prepared.

It is Sammy asleep. Do not mistake
my acceptance for resignation.

If I restrain my wanting to cup
his head in my hands and kiss his face,
it is not out of awe nor even grief.

But that this is the time of rest,
hour of tenderness, moment that will thrum
all moments to the intrepid beat
of his shadow heart, breathless

in gathering me with the other sleeping ones
awaiting the awakening.

10

On What's the Matter with "Used To"?

A couple of weeks ago, I went to breakfast with six who have been my friends the longest—since grade school and junior high. That's more than fifty years for us. And what laughs we had. Much of our conversation over fresh squeezed orange juice and eggs benedict included "used to," a phrase we didn't "used to" use a lot. But now we do. About eating, ailments, families, working, playing, sleep habits of us and our husbands. At home, still smiling, I thought, So many "used to's." And we're all still in relatively good shape. Phases. But then I thought, Into our sixth decade, we could afford, in fact, not only the nostalgia of the "used to's" but the grace of them.

For instance, last Sunday I/we had all of the family who are in town come to our house for dinner. Only eleven, I thought, easy. Just think of all the years of having a minimum of eight at every meal, on Sunday always company that made at least eleven. I remembered too having all those Sunday dinners in the dining room set with the best china and silver that had to come out of its covers and later be washed by hand. Sometimes there were even a damask cloth and napkins that would have to have any "fruit

spots" taken out by dipping in boiling water, grease spots by rub-
bing with soap in cold water before laundering. It was interesting
to remember what I used to do.

It was also lovely to think I didn't have to do that any more.
We would extend the big oak table in the kitchen, use place mats
that would wipe off, dishes and silver from the drawer, not the un-
breakable Melmac and flimsy stainless steel of years when the
children were young, but the firefly medium china and Grandma's
flatwear that I'd substituted when we were adults around the table
and putting tableware into the dishwasher.

The table could still look pretty. So could the plates, with flowers and parsley and paprika. The meal could be tasty and filling,
with turkey cooked—by Mel—on the grill outside (no roasting
pan to wash!), candied sweet potatoes in the microwave, and
Mother's date pudding baked ahead of time with only whipped
cream to spread for serving. Daughters Becky and Rinda, excellent
cooks, would bring veggies and salad; their children under five
would sit at the bar where spills wouldn't matter. I smiled thinking
how glad I was that it was now.

After dinner, instead of spending time putting all the finery
away and making sure there was not a chip, stain, or tarnish on
anything, I could go out and throw a football with my grandchildren, eight-year-old Katie now included with James, ten, Richard,
twelve, and Nicky, thirteen—the under-fives, Michael and Liska,
getting in on some tosses. The men would do the dishes since the
women prepared the meal. I could send dinner to our absent son-
in-law, Paul, gone on a real estate open house, and visit with
another, Jim, about his cases for the week.

It was a new world. A not bad one. And I wouldn't go back a
syllable. I get to say "used to" to a lot that I used to love but have
to—no, choose to—move away from now that I'm in my semi-
golden years.

But initially it's not easy. At the first suggestion of having to
give up something I've always done, especially things that I've
always loved, I resist like a stubborn, too-tired child refusing to go
to bed. Take skiing, for instance. When the good eye doctor spot-
ted the clouds drifting over my right eye injured in an accident two

years ago and said the retina could detach if I had a big jar, that I shouldn't chance skiing or waterskiing, my forever loves, I was appalled. How could I ever be a "used to" skier? On a blue sky day with new powder, stay home? Send the others off? Or on the boat on a silky lake, not take off on that slalom, cut through the froth, and play in the wake? I'd go crazy.

And then I found I wouldn't. I could look at the mountains and feel the snow under my skis, silent in a schuss as thread in cloth, or crunching on a turn like powdered sugar in a box. I could listen to tales brought home by grandsons learning to ski the tram run or daughters and sons-in-law back from the exhaustion of a day pass in flat light. I could sit on the bow of the boat and feel the spray on my ankles and calves as someone else back there tried to jump the wake or get up on one ski. It was as much fun as doing it myself.

The brain is a wonderful TV screen, complete with multiphonic sound, full color, life-size replay, to say nothing of smells and tastes and, most of all, feels. Nothing is beyond my recall, especially if what I want to call up was long ago, even far away. Names may elude me introducing my best friend, but how piano keys felt at a recital when I was a nervous ten, what a browned roast smelled like after Sunday School on the porch at the cabin, how my rattly Remington sounded when I hit the "Shift" key, how the newly developed muscles in the thighs of my first love in junior high looked as he ran for a drop shot—and now, how those skis or that ski felt on any slope or any water, I can have back on whim.

And I can be free of effort or worry or even the keen fear of not being at my best in situations that now might summon more than I have to give. Besides, I'll stay able to read and work and run around a tennis court.

"Used to"? A not bad frosting on even the plainest day.

Things That Ease the Strain

• Have a perm that's wash-and-wear, not even blow-dried. Nice. Especially since I'm a motor moron with anything but a brush. I remember too well the back-combed pouf of my young motherhood that I didn't dare even scratch and hated to sleep on and had to go to Robert Steur's college of magic twice a week for a dollar in order to stay "presentable"!

• Make peace with dieting. Maintain a comfort zone. I'm better at abstinence than moderation. Weekends and other people's food are for indulging, Mondays are for *my* fare and *my* diet. But I have to keep a sense of humor along with a sense of my proportion.

Wonderful old jokes that apply: After forty years of dieting, I should be worn on a charm bracelet. Or, the five stages of a woman's wishing: (1) to grow up, (2) to fill out, (3) to slim down, (4) to hold it in, and (5) to heck with it.

• Exercise can be the saving grace—fun exercise. Without it I wither, go stiff, am subject to injury both physical and psychological. With it I get to frolic, something easy to forget in adulthood, as I let go of whatever else might be assaulting my sense of equilibrium. And somehow it's a lot more fun with someone you can get the giggles with even as you chase a ball or walk a track or bike the neighborhood.

Every minute I save can be my own. It's so much easier to block out time for emergencies than for things I just plain want to do. Was anyone ever too busy to go to a funeral? Why not time with a very alive friend for talking about a book or going to a movie or just calling on the phone?

• Sanity must come before obligation. People respect a "circuits on overload" or "I'm on sabbatical" better than any fabricated excuse. I cannot run faster than I can—and I can do only so much, less now than I used to. Staying up all night, for instance. I used to do it once a week. In those delicious, quiet hours I'd write, read, refinish furniture, maybe even freeze raspberries. It gave me the extra "day" I always longed for, that nobody else knew about. If I kept active the next day and went to bed at a normal time, I got along just fine.

But that's not so anymore. Still tyrannized by too many and too much to love, I can get to where the too much is not "done in wisdom and order," as I try to "run faster than [I have] strength" (Mosiah 4:27). But saying no, especially to myself, is a learned ability, whose gentleness I have come to cherish almost as much as I did those all-nighters of not so long ago.

• Make friends with technology. Learning something new can replace any number of "used to's." I resisted an electric typewriter because I had loved my jumpy old portable. Then a self-correcting typewriter came along—it too took a lot of white-out to come around to. But now! Those are "used to's," and my computer is my buddy. Oh, to fix up my spelling, my typos, my uncanny aptitude for making a mistake in the very last line of a poem! My trusty Mac SE is my genie, my intrigue. The day a word processor took hold of me was another birthday.

At first an intimidating, frustrating complex of commands and errors—all mine—this amazement has become my entree to the last of my century. As have a microwave, a computer to open my car (impossible to lock in my keys!), tapes to go with me anywhere to instruct, inspire, and carry me off on words or music I heard only in lecture or concert halls even ten years ago. So much. So wondrous. If only I am willing to move on.

• Let others do what they can do as well as or better than I can. Especially now that both energy and time are becoming my most precious commodities, I must delegate, hire it out, save myself for what only I can do—and get good enough at it that what I *have* to do is what I *want* to do.

If I let it, "used to" can work for instead of against. Because that's how we were engineered to operate, through one good year, a bad season, an old skill, a new struggle—sometimes one at a time, sometimes on overlap, always in phases, abandoning what no longer makes sense. But I must stay in touch with the divine hand that sets the clock and teaches me to tell when and how. And I can, if I just pay attention, and if I am willing not to think I have to *make* everything happen nearly so much as to *let* things be.

And before it has all become "used to," I'd like to savor both the old and the new as often as possible, as I did that morning at breakfast with my oldest friends, as I do on the court or on the lake or around the block or on the phone—with those I love.

"Hello, My Friend, Hello"

My friend, let's find a way to talk
Or frolic on a court, or walk
Or take a long hour over lunch
Or in your garden pick a bunch
Of black-eyed daisies to arrange.

My friend, I need to hear from you
The sense you make and how you view
Today's pale quandaries, how you see
The puzzles fit to you, to me,
The new, the sensible, the strange.

Blessed am I with you made we,
Different from a family.
I, still the thorough wife and mother,
Daughter, matriarch, with brothers,
Find in you companion rare.

Hello, my friend, my most times wise,
Often funny, always prize
Understander, understood.
Our exchange is more than good,
It's saving grace and fresh sweet air.

11

On the Changing of the Guard

A strong woman creates a strong home that continues. My vibrant, joking friend Ruth Hinckley Willes died of cancer. For a year she had known, had battled the inevitable with surgery, chemotherapy, radiation, more surgery, would have gone on to platinum had not everything run down, run out, stopped. She was sixty-eight, younger by far than her body, central to the lives of her husband, her brothers and sisters, daughters and son, and to dozens of us who lived better in her light.

Of course we would have fought dragons to have her stay. But then again, the dragon conquered would have meant her staying, the pain, the blighted expecting, the lessening of her powers to be herself.

In the hospital watching her sleeping deeply one morning near the end, the machines bubbling and blinking, the tubes snaking liquid life into her, I thought, Ruth, it's time, isn't it?

I thought of how she'd sallied through life straightening pictures and perspectives, fixing meals and psyches, arranging a sense of direction with a sense of humor. And you've become a presence,

I thought—asleep or awake, you're a presence. You always will be. I leaned close to her cheek to tell her and said only, "I love you." She did not stir, barely opened her eyes for a moment and said, "Yes."

Yes, I thought. Yes to you and your saying yes to the rest of us. Yes Yes Yes.

I remembered a typical lesson of hers in Relief Society, the Mormon women's organization meeting once a week. It was in the chapel to accommodate the crowd, and it must have been about self-approval. To illustrate how much each of us was and how little we knew of the unique worth of each other, she had us take turns coming to the pulpit to introduce ourselves in a way I'll never forget: in no more than two minutes, by our maiden names and by what we do best.

It was fascinating. One after another we women, some of whom had lived in the same ward for thirty years, came alive as a whole new kind of creatures. One woman was a maker of dolls, another a docent for the zoo. One said she was an excellent listener, one that she painted on an easel in her bedroom. But even more revealing than our specialties were the personalities that shone from under those maiden names. We were different, all right, even the younger ones young again, our identities emblazoned on us not in any role, but as very particularized individuals. One woman, then eighty-two, had married at sixty-five, glowed with telling us how she was the same before and after, always a teacher, though she had been regarded so differently after having "Mrs." in front of her name.

At the end of the parade, Ruth said, "You see, we're more than our status, far more than our age. We are one-at-a-time children of God, the same as we were as girls. And each of us makes a home." She filled a lifetime with making that clear.

The night after that visit to the hospital when her daughter called to say that the family had decided she had struggled enough, mostly for them, and that they were taking away all but the oxygen and morphine, I wept. But when I saw her sinking deeper and deeper into sleep over the next few days, in no apparent pain, willing, sweetly ready, kin to some force beyond that hospital room or knowing, I knew. Translucent, her face stilled to youngness, her slim lovely hands that had soothed fevers and sensibilities now resting only on each other, I knew it was time, a deserved and generous time.

I knew she knew it too. Now when I bent to put my cheek to hers, to speak my words into her ear, her eyes did not open, but her lips, parted in sleep, closed, and from her throat came soft sounds that said in a language beyond my interpreting but not beyond my grasp, "Yes, yes." She said it crooning, gurgling, like a baby first learning to make sounds. And I said yes too. To her and to a loving God to whom time and stages and readiness were particles in a very different perspective.

While the gap will be wide and the wound severe for everyone who occupied her kitchen and living rooms over the years, Ruth's keeping of her house lent itself to letting go. She lived each stage and age to its fullest, never looked back in yearning or remorse. Once she said to me when I was thirty-nine and she was fifty, "Emma Lou, fifty is the best of all. Just you wait, you'll see." She was right. Eleven years ahead of me in everything, Ruth knew how to be mentor as well as friend.

But the greatest teaching she ever did was to show me, as she showed her remarkable family and the women she taught, that home is within us, that the divine spark of ourselves is beyond time and circumstance.

Ruth's home continued because her eighty-one-year-old husband took over as homemaker. He knew how—to cook a stew, make a bed, do a wash. He brought home from the store that first night after the funeral the biggest box of Tide I've ever seen, as if he were planning to wash the world and had plenty of time to do it.

That house continued to be a home, not so much because of the Tide, but because Joe made sure that life continued. He wrote Ruth's life story, having completed dozens already for older friends. Till he died two years later, he worked in his marigolds and roses, sang with his great-grandchild, put on his sweatsuit and walked around a dozen blocks taking stories and sweet cherries to neighbors as he went. He was much more than a survivor.

As was Ruth. When my mother died, Ruth and Joe came to plant a rose in our backyard. When Ruth died, her children brought to me her African violets. In death, life. The continuing, according to the gospel of Ruth Hinckley Willes and how she kept her home.

Matriarch

Center of the wheel, matrix, she will not be gone.
Her hands that warmed the other hands,
shook salt into sameness,
rubbed shine into what had to be done
are far from cold.
Her eyes that stayed open for other eyes,
knew tears and how to give hers
to take others' away are seeing.
Her feet that sprang to run down
a hungering, to trample a threat
quietly go about their business.
Her breath that breathed sun
into trying and green into discouragement
touches where it's needed.
Her ears that drew sadness
away from what was left
are denied no hearing,
still give laughing audience to laughing.
Her heart will not be closed on
its numberless passions
and indignations.
Her amazing head has not
gone off with its secrets.
Her soul, transparent, will not be replaced
by a vacant moon.

No. I will hold to how she filled her spaces,
recognize her in the strong fingers of a daughter
finding the right note,
see her in the run of a grandson heading out,
feel her in a friend weeping in private.
I will follow her abundance into aromas
of pinion and cinnamon,
the ripe cold of a spring.

Her house will not empty.
Band-Aids and soup,
peppermints and a paintbrush,
much-handled books
will speak for her.

God will send autumn and Christmas,
then of course summer
and let us hear her singing us home.

And someone will be carrying on.

12

On Going It Together—and Alone

The Preparation

A committee can be much more than the sum of its parts. I miss as much as anything in these empty nest years having my "committee" preparing for something. I remember on that Saturday in December in 1981, when we were trying to get ready for Dinny's farewell. At twenty-two our tall blonde fourth daughter had elected to go on a mission, would learn to speak French and to pedal a bicycle in a skirt for eighteen months in Toulouse near the Pyrenees, one of thirty thousand volunteer missionaries proseletyzing for The Church of Jesus Christ of Latter-day Saints—the Mormons.

There had been shopping and soul-searching, wrenching and being put together. Tomorrow church would be a program including all of her family, music and talks preceding the real farewells that would be at a gathering at our house for over a hundred kith and kin.

Saturday was the countdown. Mel made three trips to the store. A friend came by with flowers, sisters-in-law and cousins and neighbors with cookies. The phone rang and rang again. Dinny's talk emerged for her in neat black typing on white paper while mine sprawled in scribbles on orange scraps beside my bed.

But my daughters and I had all come back to the kitchen that had warmed and fed us for thirty years—except for Rinda, who with Jim, James, and Katie was one thousand two hundred and forty-two miles away. The air of tomato and bouillon and peppercorns and basil, chocolate and butterscotch ran us all together that day and into the night before the morning of. Shelley was making Dream Bars, a house specialty for all of her life. Megan spread butter and Parmesan cheese over bread sticks cut by Dinny to be baked to golden at the last minute, while Becky whipped up batches of a friend's marshmallow brownies and I replaced old candles from Christmas in the dining room while brewing the soup. Twenty-one-month-old Grace sat on the counter and sampled uncooked dough just as her mother had, twenty-four years before.

All our lives we'd bumped bottoms in the kitchen, trying to do fifteen things at once. For dinners when they were little, for parties when they were bigger, for birthdays, holidays, after-school days, before-boating days, we'd been that committee getting ready. In the noisy commotion, we had learned of each other's deepest concerns and lightest considerations. We'd stirred and mashed and cubed and browned our way through tests and boyfriends, hairstyles and testimonies, testimonies of faith private enough not to be voiced in even the church meeting of fasting worshippers designated once a month for that purpose. The kitchen and being busy allowed an ease not common to other grounds.

At first, of course, it was messier than it was profitable to have five little sets of fingers in my every pie. But the littler they were, the more interested they were in "helping." So they learned to help. And over the years that help turned into blessing indeed for any culinary enterprise. Those hands could do in fifteen minutes what mine alone could never have done in half a day. And in the fixings, they found themselves occupied—with savory inducements to smile and make do and walk tall and eat hearty of all that came out of a kitchen or went into our making it as a team. Saturday was another hectic and happy experiment in putting it all together with wooden spoons and sifters and pastry brushes.

In any kitchen anywhere for the rest of our lives, we'll be doing it by committee, the six of us. Just as I will season with my mother's dashes of nutmeg and my grandmother's sprinkles of sage, they'll carry into their cupboards and onto their stoves and tables the festive know-how of having learned, bottom to bottom, in a crowded kitchen. As I do in the now often empty kitchen where I still feel their drips and spills like laughter on a conversation in the quietest preparation of the smallest meal.

The Clearing Up

Epilogue to the preparations and the party has to to be the cleanup. In housekeeping, it can be exhausted duty—or wistful unwinding.

The big day comes and goes, a glory. The open house celebrating Dinny's being, her leaving, lasts long and the family lingers longer, their staying the postponement we all look for. But they go, all of them, the ones at home quietly to bed.

All but me. I want them gone. I want this time for my task, my safe reentry. At 3:00 A.M., the early morning of the night, comes the beginning of the decompression. The physicality of exit. With everyone else asleep, I attack with quiet ardor and order the aftermath. I scrape and wash and dry. I sort and pat, store, and cover. The china I rub and stack knowing each piece has been rubbed and stacked in exactly the same way by Mother and Grandma, probably with the same sense of letting down, moving about in the settling of festivities and certainties. The rituals of routine are as comforting as cool sheets.

It would have been jovial and comradely to do it all as I almost always have, with my husband or daughters, talking over the party, the conversations, the food. But this night there is regeneration in being alone, in regrouping the parts, reassembling the ableness. I am doing what I know how to do for people I know how to love. I am also doing what I like to do, have liked since I first made smooth white sauce, found that a stuffed olive wrapped in bacon was better than either one apart, felt the pride of having my father praise my chocolate pudding or my mother the way I arranged jelly glasses in perfect rows in the fruit room. For more than fifty years I have liked the process of making a house, a meal, a family work.

And now, for really the first time, I am realizing what that process gives back to me. A sorting time. A building time. A decompressing time. In not actually having to think about what I am about, in the sweet inconsideration of that unconscious competence, I can both relish and move on. After a party or a funeral, at the end of a test week or a honeymoon, a trip or a mission, after a holiday or after having a baby, after a stay as a hostage or a parade as a celebrity, anyone needs it—the letting down, the recovery by rote.

In a while I will leave the kitchen gleaming and straight. I will exit this chamber whole and well cleansed myself, tired in healthy ways, ready for sleep. And in the morning it will be there to receive me and mine, its practices, havoc, and return to order part of an ongoingness that will never fail.

To a Daughter About to Become a Missionary
For Dinny

Twenty-two, she sleeps upstairs
between the windows of my life,
in the sleigh bed that has housed
the comings of four generations

like exotic potted plants chosen
to color bedrooms with blossoming.
Two high birdseye dressers contain her,
drawers closed on pink turtlenecks

and Speedos, walls of rackets and mustachioed
smiles. Mirrors swing her reflection
of medicated soap and squashed rollers
dropping away from night to issue

a daytime Pieta laughing and grieving,
beautifully turned out, surprising as
a crocus in snow. Other rights postponed,
the child that God intended will wear

the sanctity of the blue blazer,
skirted and frocked, innocent in her
expectation. Of course we have known
she would leave, the covers

opened and closed. It is time.
The horizon whitens. Water runs.
This is morning. She will see. France
will tell. She is changing to

the garments of The Word, will take on
the terrors of the verb To Be,
not knowing yet why departure
spells return. Five hundred forty-seven

and a half-days. She will open wide
her arms sweatered for the long cold.
The darkness will lighten and she will become
the waiting room for the willing stranger.

Kisses blow like blizzards through my empty
spaces saying, God, please. I go up to sit on
her suitcase that will not close,
press messages into her shoes,

the smell of kitchen under the leather
of her scriptures. Snow has made feathers

of trees. She lifts the sleepy shadow
of her face, steps into the air. She is gone.

I do not dare breathe in the bedroom.
Or move. Only to listen to the runners
of the sleigh bed following her.

And me unable to touch it for fear
of blanketing the sweet shiny smell
of Dr. Pepper lip gloss beneath the down,
above the furrows of knees along the floor.

13

On the Other Home:
Our Mt. Air Cabin

Keeping the cabin is more than either sustenance or launching. It is life itself, old, essential, natural. Being part of that is like having Mother, Father, Grandma, and all my children and grandchildren in on my every day being alive.

For as long as I can remember, I have spent summers in "Our" Canyon. As a girl I lived there with my mother and father and brothers and cousins from the day school was out in the spring until it opened in the fall. Grandma lived in her cabin just around the mountain from ours, and when she didn't have her friends up, I got to sleep in the cot across the room from her magic breathing. Her cabin became ours after she died when I was twelve, and until 1975 we shared it with my brothers' families, by then thirty-six of us, which meant only three spread-out weeks from June to September to be in the place where we loved most to be.

In that year I wrote my first novel, *Never Past the Gate*, about initiation, the discovery of good and evil through our adventures there as children of nature and invention. So much to love! So much to learn by, to want carried on for our children and theirs!

And so we built our own cabin up the mountain with views of all the old haunts and hikes of that wondrous childhood.

In 1976, when the cabin was just finished, I ended a poem, "The Building," with:

> Many parts of my life go without notice.
>
> The cabin grows and is itself
> in the oldest place we know.
>
> It alone is unawed by what it says.
> It stands on its own feet,
> wears warm fittings over its spine
> and kisses the arena of Mt. Air Canyon.
>
> Now we can rest. This is the cabin:
>
> For all to come, all we will need will be time:
>
> what it needs now is a chance to blossom.
> And that will come
> under the snow
> and in the spring.

This is how it continues to work, housekeeping at the cabin, the meshing of generations and impulses, recorded in this sampling of some things let loose on my old portable typewriter in my study there:

Saturday morning, November 17, 1979. Cabin! I am alone in this wonder of a crow's nest, silky and collected at last, snug in the brown arms of this place, watching the white sky move and the towers of trees hold still, against their grey base. Only in the hollows is the rusty remaindering of fall. The rest is the color of the granite spines and mountain mahogany, and pine spikes are islands of black green in the oyster wash. Soon it will snow and all will be the color of the white sky.

This home lives on stilts with its head in the pines, a screened porch to eat on, enough beds for all, a shower and an outdoor loo, a living room and a balcony with lengths of jack pine for a railing, and clerestory windows taking on the sky and the mountains— and this study, my tree house on the upper corner where every childhood escapade can pop into view.

Last night for a quick dinner, Mel and I struggled up the slick hill in a couple of inches of snow and a skiff of ice with supplies for the root cellar, thinking this might be our last time to make a run. He lugged in sacks of canned goods and quarts of drinks, I paper goods and Pinesol, new brown work gloves, batteries, apples, and cereal, both of us with papers and books to read, lessons to prepare, and a talk to be thought about.

We had our creamy mushroom soup and toast with some hot cider and cinnamon rolls, with sliced apple. No matter the fare, so much better somehow than at home. While Mel unloaded and settled, contented, into his paper, I got to spend the evening doing what he knows I love—puttering, indigenous as a little squirrel with its pinecone to work on: tacking more batting to secure the Visqueen around the dining room, chopping wonderful tangy wood, emptying cold ashes up the mountain, building magnificent fires that in two hours sent us from twenty-eight degrees to sixty-five—by the thermometer on the outside living room wall. And the maintaining of it! Selecting the wood and coal by size and compactness for starting or adding, watching the blaze, adding a heaping teaspoon of Blue Devil to ssss blue and yellow and take after the soot in the two-story chimney. "Who chops his own wood is twice warmed" indeed.

Scheherazade on the old scratchy stereo. All the time the talk or no talk, the comfortableness of its not mattering which. The belonging. The thinking as I go. The finally slow, sleepy reading of the paper in the big overstuffed chair from my girlhood. The going to bed. The shedding of layers never worn at home. Mel asleep for an hour or two before me, warm, unperplexed. Cold prayers, more sure, less ardent than at home. The cool warmth of sheet blankets and quilts. Now the having succumbed to an electric blanket, the unwillingness to turn my side on. The going to sleep too fast, never enough soaking in, the dark branch outside the big window next to the bed lifting me toward Castle Crags and Mother and Father. And Stan? Mel's salty, solid brother dead at age fifty-seven last week of cancer—are they finding each other? As I will find them . . . between . . . sleeping and . . .

Then the waking. The far-off ticking, then chiming, of the clock that disappeared somewhere in the night. The seeping in of no light, only a lightening—of covers, of outlines, of the shape of windows. It's 7:12 by my watch. Sunrise. Sky grey-blue behind pines, clerestories, pink across the Indian feathers of trees on the ridge. The fiery arch of mandarin rainbow. Darker orange, then peach, apricot, spreading from intense light at its base. Then bronze. Golden. Yellow. The clock ticking it away. Diffuse. Lavender blurring of edges that become pale pink-grey clouds beyond the bowing of pine branches, rhythmic in the gradual paling, diminishing pink absorbed by blue. The clock striking 7:30. The horizon barely different from the sky. The pink gone. Everything ice blue. Mel still sleeping, for him a delicious rarity.

For me, how often a chance to include a sunrise in a day? Almost always, I'm up to my list mentality, so much I contrive to do. But at the cabin a whole different pace, everything like part of the weather, simply happening. And suppose there would never be another sunrise? How would I have felt about those eighteen minutes? It is that absolute acquaintance with return that allows my equanimity in loss. At the cabin I take time to think about what is in a sunrise, a night, a day. Nice.

Now it is ten o'clock. Back to activity. But a gentle kind. I have hammered plastic over the picnic table out on the flat by the bonfire pit, poured new antifreeze in the drains, built a fine fire in the kitchen, made a Roman Meal breakfast with butter and brown sugar for Mel and me, using supplies stocked here for the winter, done dishes in a cupful of water from the teakettle, been captivated and calmed by the oldest of routine nonroutine.

After his longest sleep in how long?—so good for him—Mel has gone to business in the city that at least for the next three hours will claim no part of me. He likes it, the city, as much as the cabin, likes his busy job with constant people. Once in a while, so do I. But this morning, I wouldn't trade with him for the world. Certainly not for this soft world. This has to be the home that even heaven could find ways to let happen again and again in any season there might be.

And the keeping of it, for me—effort? Struggle? As simple and right as smoke floating up from chimneys still hot from the red coals saying we've been here.

Friday, June 25, 1982, 4:45 P.M. *already! Cabin!* Too quickly, that's how it works. This morning at the cabin I was lying in the woolly blankets watching the sun color the white sky, trying to whistle back to the bird that called whoo-oooo over and over outside the long window opened for the first time of the summer that came very late.

We had come up—just the two of us, Richard, five, and I—a late spree for his birthday. He started the day, in bed beside me, by asking, "When will we have our hammering contest, Gramma Grey?"

By eleven we had hammered a dozen ten-penny nails into the old stump, whittled two flipper crotches from kinnikinnick—what a word to say!—by the creek, strained dirt for mud pies, cut rhubarb from between the logs in the retaining wall, eaten canyon soft eggs with the spoons on our pocket knives, sugared and cooked the rhubarb along with crusty brown bread pudding after building a slow fire in the kitchen stove and splitting a little kindling from the aspen rounds stacked in the wood closet.

By time for lunch, which was cheese melted on canyon toast in the black oven and apple juice from the fridge, it had started to rain. Clouds bumped themselves into thunder and we noticed that the barbed lightning over Pine Top was always followed by crashes and then the gentle downpour of a June storm that would clear for sure by 3 or 4.

We postponed our hike to the spring to see the place where the creek got its start, instead pulled out the scrapbook his Great-Grandmother Warner made for me starting in 1926, pictures cut

from *Saturday Evening Posts* of Campbell Kiddies, Norman Rock-
well's Boy Scouts, Hiawatha, a prim damsel waiting for her beau.
We listened to a record his mother had listened to over and over,
Sally Terry singing "Scarlet Ribbons" and "The Fox on the Town-
O." It was wonderful work, being a mama again to a small child in
the canyon in June.

He was full of questions like "Who built this cabin?" And
when I showed him the blueprints and said his Uncle Bruce
Markosian had designed it, he said, "I don't believe you,
Gramma," and ran up the mountain, came back with the screen
door slamming behind him, nodding, and said, "Yep. From up
there it does look like those pictures Bruce drawed." So we had a
swing in the hammock and wondered how that bat last summer
got in.

Between escapades, I swept around the stoves, watered primroses, slicked up the kitchen sinks, taught him how to miter corners making our bed. The cabin shone in direct proportion to how
little we did, Richard and I getting happier and dirtier by the job
and by the minute. Nice work. Happy work.

But by two, I began to get itchy. The day was wearing away.
Too quickly it would be time to go back to the city, back to a meeting, another house to clean, wash to do, dinner to fix, a night out
at the movies or whatever Mel would choose—maybe tennis with
some friends—all good, no, exhilarating and satisfying things, but
ohhhh. The day would be gone. And I would not have read the
rest of that play by a friend, written the letter to a missionary
daughter, put in my journal any of the fullness of the day, not even
read the newspapers I am hired to read, let alone sat with a
thought for a single minute. Little wonder, I muse, that mothering
and wifing and keeping the house and its occupants, even so happily, can shave away a lifetime. Little wonder we begin to know
what time it is by the sinking of the sun. And the sinking of spirits
because it is too soon.

Still, in the canyon, everything is different, even time. And
often it is the combining of the thinking and the doing, the perfect
mixture.

Of course it comes full circle, right up to the present, the cabin and its treasures. And the keeping of it as a house and as the holder of sustenance and balm:

Tuesday, May 26, 1987, Memorial Day weekend. Yesterday Sammy spent his second month birthday with us opening the cabin for the season. The night before yesterday, Memorial Day — or Decoration Day as we used to call it — Mel and I had visited the three-foot grave in a new memorial park out south under Mount Olympus. Sod had begun to green over the square of turf, a very new shined-up metal marker declaring simply, "Samuel Thayne Rich, Born March 25, 1987, Died March 25, 1987." We left wild roses, red, in a bud vase by his name and went off to put in supplies for the twelve who would be coming to the cabin on a stormy holiday to take down winter plastic on the screened porch, vacuum and mop, clean out flies and cobwebs, get the water line running, clean cupboards and closets, scour the sink and the old tub, rake a leafy path to the bonfire pit, put sweet-smelling fresh sheet blankets on eight beds, fill the bird feeders. Summer would be here; we needed to be ready.

For all of my sixty-two years, opening the cabin has been Memorial Day. The May after the February that Father died at fifty-nine, Mother had us four children and our growing families putting up the chimneys, tacking rugs on the porch, emptying wood boxes in the kitchen. A visit to the cemetery she regarded as totally superfluous. "This is where he'd want us to be, laughing and mopping and slicking up for summer where we all know he is, not out there long-faced by a grave and paying attention to where we know he isn't." How others did was fine too. "Different families do different things" was how she often explained our uniquenesses without diminishing the doings of others.

The May after Mother died fifteen years later, there we all were, by then probably close to forty of us, doing the same opening of the cabin on Memorial Day, seeing her in her paint smock engineering the wiping out of cupboards and the bringing out of the green wicker rockers from the stack of mattresses on her bed by the black Monarch stove in the living room. We liked it and we knew she did, and Father. It was celebration, confirmation, continuity in action.

Always Memorial Day included a hike with my Scoutmaster brother Homer when the jobs were done and then a bonfire with hot dogs on whittled sticks and marshmallows browned to a caramel perfection, sometimes a sleep-over with wall-to-wall cousins and the pungence of smoke and pine gum in unshowered hair, the cool breath of the creek singing under the tongue-in-groove floors, the giggling into the night and the not-so-quiet desperation of parents wanting sleep.

In the twelve years since we built our own cabin up the hill and two brothers bought their own down the road, we've never missed opening on Memorial Day, nor remembering, in every light turned on and window washed, the convivial splendor of what Mother and Father taught us to do by heart.

Yesterday it was much the same. With only two of our five families here to plant pansies and impatiens by the front ramp and shake quilts over the deck railing, the twelve of us took longer than usual to heft and pat the place into shape. Especially since six of the twelve were like the runaway kids we used to be when we sidled out of Father's attacking of the woodpile to run the water line and check on last winter's snowslides. Slippery they were, those six of ten grandchildren in town for the opening, and having the time of their lives, their parents issuing mandates, we grandparents not especially nonplussed by their not being heard.

By evening, after a wet bonfire where drooping black marshmallows tasted just fine, evening fell like the intermittent rain to find us gathered as always around the fire in the tall black stove, with me passing out pink peppermints and promising to draw, for the littlest to guess at, pictures with M&Ms. One daughter was at the piano, another on the violin playing hymns like "Our Mountain Home So Dear," songs from *The Sound of Music*, and then from *Fiddler on the Roof*, "Where are you going, my little one, little one? Where are you going, my baby, my own? Turn around and she's two, turn around and she's four. Turn around and she's a young girl going out of the door." I took my sad happy tears to the kitchen to listen to them, waiting for the last verse, "Turn around and she's a young wife with babes of her own."

Seven-year-old Katie read stories on the bed to her two-year-old sister, Liska, and her four-year-old cousin Michael, who was wearing a canyon snuggle bunny like his mother wore thirty years before. Son-in-law Paul sat in the big overstuffed chair from my childhood home, writing notes on meditation. Another, Jim, hooked up a new light in the kitchen. Grampa Mel played checkers with thirteen-year-old Nicky, who scorned the chopping and hammering of his eleven-year-old brother, Richard, and ten-year-old cousin, James, both too young and involved to come in and out of the rain until gone for.

On the first page of a new guest log I'd brought from my trip to Russia, the twelfth since the hand-pouring of the footings for the cabin in 1975, I wrote "Happy Memorial Day, Family! Here we are."

And there we were. All of us. Mother, Father, my brothers and families, even Grandma, whose cabin had been opened in the same fashion decades before I was born. To say nothing of our family now, the three girls away this year with families and perspectives of their own, all, I was very sure, in on the opening.

And Sammy. The marker out there by the filling-in grass only a naming of a place. He was in the place that would be his along with us on every opening and closing of the cabin or of a season for as long as pines might choose to take on the sky and mountains to be there to climb.

Planting Wildflowers in September at the Cabin

Easy, say directions on the can:
Scatter, rake, or stomp in gently,
spray/sprinkle till damp, not wet.

Too easy? Unbelievable?
Not to the delighter in how.

The moist seeds, webbed in the floss
of each other's company, buried alive,
come out with my fingers
winged, Gypsy-ready for somewhere
new.

Shaggy, hung with their own marsh
and mountains, they cling to my
fingers,
scatter like kisses on the brown hillside.

I rake them in, say,
Live here, tantalize spring.

I will return again and again,
my palms wet with you,
my nails sprouting your musky scent.

And flowers, surely flowers,
wild as gentian and Indian paintbrush,
will grow from my fingertips,
silky bouquets to touch across my face.

And I will rise to them
no matter where I am.

14

On Not Forgetting to Like It

Enough of life I am captive to, but doing what I want is mostly liking what I do. So much of it can seem obligatory—having to do—from watering plants that will die, to throwing out leftovers that already have. From putting on a face—oh, why did my daughters get me onto eye stuff?—to balancing a checkbook—I gave up long ago, just estimate, even that a nuisance. From filling out forms to wiping off fingerprints. The worst—defrosting a freezer whose door has been left open, or cleaning the storage room where everyone's excess has been dropped.

It's easy to get caught in the futility of repetition and the insistence of duty that plague any housekeeping. Days can disappear and nights be spent in agonizing over what has to be done. And in envying or being discouraged because someone else seems to be doing exactly what a dream life would suggest—nothing but what makes absolute sense and brings total joy.

Like my son-in-law Jim. His voice sounded boyish, excited: "I've been working sixteen-hour days—and nights, Grey. I guess I've never been more exhausted or more happy." He was calling on the phone from the hospital telling about his plastic surgical residency that was about to end, his last months being spent under the benign tyranny of a master surgeon bent on his residents going into practice as the best—and most tired—in the business. Jim's final months of training had been not unlike his internship in the emergency room, except that now it was not fifteen simple operations in twelve hours, but maybe one tough, tough one in fifteen hours—like making a new arm out of a fibula and skin from a thigh.

"Isn't it something, though," I say, "at thirty-five to be doing exactly what you dreamed of doing at five—every day of your life getting up to knowing you'll get to go out and do precisely that?"

Then I think, But look what it's taken to get there. Sixteen years beyond high school, with hundred-hour weeks, days of no eating, nights of no sleep, a family wondering sometimes who he might be.

Still, there it is, that life now of doing exactly what he loves, day after day, and having the life the rest of us do in between.

I shake my head in a little envy, then think, Hey, wait a minute, Lulie. Beyond and around the basics, you can get to do what you like to do—every day. But you have to remember to like what you like. And never forget any of it.

I start the day with for instances: It's easy to make tapioca without remembering to smell the vanilla. A grandson on the project never will forget—once you've showed him. To put the sugar in by pinches to feel the grains. To thump the nutmeg in rusty splotches on the pale yellow fluff. To listen to the hollow collision of the pitcher against the bowl or the foamy softness of the pouring, and then taste the froth as it slips past your teeth from the spoon, nutmeg granules the last to go, spicy as spring on the nose. That boy understands what I mean. It's not a job if it's honored by noticing.

When the sink is cleared, I remember, I'll bet it'll make a difference to use some Ajax on the poor old stainless steel that's spent most of its twenty-nine years barely up from stainless. And make it a point to remember how much you like the smell of Ajax and the relieved gleam of a just-scoured anything. I still did.

And so there was more.

That morning the sun was out for the first time in weeks. A beam came through the full-length stained glass window that our daughter Becky had made us for Christmas—yellow, bright green, grey-blue. Had I forgotten about color? About the playing of dust on a ray in a Monday morning front hall stacked with laundry to go downstairs, coats to be cleaned, books to be put away. I told myself, Take time for the prisms.

I was able to walk into, even through, the room where the night before, grandchildren had pulled puppets and tea party doings across the view of snackers and watchers. I remembered Mother's teaching me, "Pick up at night, be glad in the morning." I was. I liked the neatness, the having put things right on my way to bed. Easy, I thought. My house was coming to attention, my attention. I felt the calm exuberance of order. I was doing exactly what I liked to do.

Then I was in my Fiesta, my filthy little Plum. I drove to the car wash, inserted my dollar bill in the change machine, Washington up, was entranced that four quarters dropped like coins from heaven. Into the magic stall, with quarters deposited, the wand in my hand, I shot suds. I could wave the spray anywhere. The mud and salt sloshed off, off, and away—in white bubbles! Then the rinse, the glimmer, the toweling. The unfamiliar triumph—after a lifetime of five-foot-two—of finally being able to reach across the top of anything. Then driving off noticing the back window even, reflecting. Keep track of how, I told myself.

Driving, I thought, I love to do this, drive—have since I sneaked the car at fifteen. And now with my music on—just *La Traviata* and me in our little cocoon. I never tire of it. I've been doing a whole lot of things I just plain want to do. And just because the whole day is not totally of my choosing, I forget how much of it can be. Sure, I'll have to stay up or get up when I'd rather be sleeping, and be in a meeting when I'd rather be writing. There will never be a truce in the battle to find more time to play tennis or talk to friends or to my family. And ready or not, six o'clock will come and the kitchen will need me.

But, I promise myself, I'll keep in mind noticing what I love in whatever I do. Especially in those minutes when I get to get to my work, when I get to write. While I do, through the whole wonderful birthing of whatever, I'll be noticing how the keys feel under my fingers, how exciting the shotgun spurts on the page—now screen—that bring up words I would never have thought to put together, how cleansing the stripping of ideas to whatever shape they take outside my head, on paper. Even with its frustrations, its too-often puny producings, its compelling entreaties, I will know the satisfaction of wanting to work.

And play, I tell myself. When you drink some cranberry juice or dunk a graham cracker in milk, feel them go. Taste water. Notice how your knees go upstairs. Move somewhere fast enough to perspire and then love the heat and coolness, the opening of pores. Enjoy anticipation and preparing. The smell of chicken on the grill. The texture of Borden's sweetened condensed milk in anything. Going to sleep in a warm bed with a cool pillow. Reading next to someone to mention a fact to, the drowsy moments when your prayers have been said and your worries tucked into them, the brash reminder of the cuckoo three rooms away, the aching of the furnace, the smell of soap, and the snapping off of the light, the finding of the perfect fit. And then morning, again and again—morning. Make it matter by noticing, I tell myself.

By then, driving to the store with the list I'd put off paying attention to, I stopped having to tell myself anything. It was telling me. Beyond the cruel press of not enough time, not enough resources, too much demand, too little wherewithal, I actually can be in command enough to figure out how to be getting to do exactly what I want. Over and over. Between and around and under all the things I guess I really wouldn't choose at all.

But then again, what are they? Some days I can't even remember. Other days, of course, it's all I can do to forget.

Hedonist

You can do what the moment occasions.
You can function as spirit demands.

Today you're not hard put for reasons
To follow your heart, head, or hands.

Have a day of the life hedonistic
With being a woman away
From anything slightly domestic.
"Carpe diem!" you smile—"seize the day!"

Oh, rash and delicious the options,
The resources, wonders to tap:
Read a book, see a show, hear an opera!
And what do you take? Yep—a nap.

15

On Making a Home for One

Not all homes are houses. All homes need keeping. One person can equal a home. I recall a morning in the sunny apartment of Edith, a teacher/student/friend who lives alone. It is small and has a spare orderliness about it, a peace and an energy. A thick hand-thrown plate glazed brown is a shade lighter than the fresh bran cookies she hands me, still warm, their rich, molasses-tanged sweetness the strongest aroma in the kitchen.

Across the room from me are four cupboards with glass knobs, glass panels, and metal catches. Inside I see a Betty Crocker cookbook, five unmatching plates standing against the wall, a brass pepper grinder from India, a miniature pressure cooker from Italy, a blown glass butterfly, the compact edition of the *Oxford English Dictionary*, a box of stationery, a file of notes, and a glass orange juicer.

From the top of the cupboard, an impatiens plant leafs down inquisitively, a Christmas card of children who are black, white, yellow, and brown presents its wreath serenely, and an unruly bunch of baby's breath makes a bouffant ball.

We have had an hour of nonstop talking—about her classes, our writing, the people who are important in our lives, the celebration that spring is making outside the windows. Now we are comfortably silent. I watch her hands as she takes the last cookie sheet from the thirty-one-year-old range, slides the cookies onto a narrow yellow shelf, puts the pan in the browned suspended sink.

The scent of our rose hip–mint tea begins to curl above the air of the cookies. She is as much at home in her kitchan as all of these objects, but home is somehow more than the sum of these dear parts. Through the door I see another windowsill, a soft, scarred wooden monk from Guatemala, photographs of her brother looking at flowers, of Matthew, three, and Luke, seven months, and pictures of the Oriental children of a friend in Japan.

Neither arranged nor cluttered, the spaces of Edith's living announce and allow her loves: Above the sink are postcards of a mosque in Egypt through iron filigree, a photograph of fishermen on the Nile with the tombs of Luxor in the distance. Around the stove are a white General Electric kitchen clock as old as I am, two handmade plaid hotpads on hooks, an improbable wok from Holland. In the window an Indian medicine wheel designed by her sister-in-law, a crystal prism—making rainbows—from her boyfriend's cabin in Marble Mountain, a cyclamen in first bloom, a Coptic cross from Egypt, a rock from an Iowa quarry, a fragile section of a wasp's nest. Nothing is without its own history or Edith's affection. Everything has been touched by the grace of belonging.

No husband, no children, no roommates. None of the people we think we must homemake for. Yet this is undeniably a home and Edith undeniably a homemaker.

And how many "single" women do I know who are central to their larger families? Each a confidante, a rescuer, a giver of solace and funding, housing and parties, a provider of solidity in time of stress and division? Typical was my great-aunt Kate Stayner, who never married but who furnished my brothers and me with surprise and adventure as well as the most comfortable overnight lodgings any of us could ever have imagined, with a bath in what was almost unknown in our childhood—hot water to our ears. A professional woman in a time when few were, she operated her own advertising agency. Her office in the old Bishops' Building on Main Street held mystery and fun—a typewriter, a roll-down desk, an exit from a fire escape outside her window. More, in her Kensington apartment she offered us, and all the rest of our huge family, the camaraderie of being understood and extravagantly cared for. It was there we went to take our naps. What more telling compliment to comfort? What disregard for human worthwhileness when such as Aunt Kate or Edith are relegated to lesser status simply because they make that home by themselves!

On Edith's bulletin board above the phone is a neatly typed quote from William Stafford, American poet: "Be here so well that even one time is often." What caring, what offhand diligence has made that invitation a reality! Nothing is too new to be welcome. Nothing is too old to stay. So different from my Aunt Kate, so much the same.

Perhaps it is the same revelation of love and loving that Edith has used to turn three rooms into a home. Perhaps it is because she knows it matters that even a casual guest, there for a day, can enter and be home.

———— ❧ ————

The Other Side
For Another Friend

Single, bent by guilt on pleasing,
she is there too well, unseparate. She
lives alone with tasks and pleasures
inhabited by unborn children and
the lives of others, rarely her own.

The home she furnishes is redolent of
her perfumed warm spots,
Diet Coke and brussel sprouts
her passing fare. Plants get watered, visible

tops dusted. Naturally alive to the same
terrors of not enough she is enough.

The solitary radiates and howls
in her. Her bath and bed seem monologues,
her departures without plot. Predators
assume she has time so she goes
to sleep late, past tired, having done.

She occupies home with the hard-won ardor
of having no one else to do, only her
to trample or realize a dream or let go
what is hers to keep. And love. And run
for: In her privacy the sweet unknown.

16

On Movin' On

Saturday, December 13, last year was not easy. It was the day to put up Christmas. And I did not like it.

It started in an empty house. Never had Christmas come quietly, so having not a soul around to breathe it in and put it up was more than strange. Mel had to go to a meeting, and three out of our five daughters lived away. The other two had busy days of their own just as I had had at their stage, with young children and preseason rushing to do it all.

Mel set the quite beautiful, pungent fir in the usual corner and dashed through the path of its needles inhaling his skim milk and banana on his way to the car, waving.

And there we were, the tree and I, in that quiet chaos, wondering what in the world to do with each other.

Music. That had to be the answer. Turn through the house the 1962 stereo, played till it needed pliers to work its switches. Out with the Christmas records, the choir, the strings of the Philharmonic, Barbra Streisand, the Carpenters. They were warm and scratched with familiarity. And they were a disaster. In their grooves lay little girl voices and candles for Santa, Patty Play Pals and new skis, bikes painted in secret places, beds refinished for surprises on Christmas morning.

"Joy to the World" rang through another time. I was in the same house getting ready for our moving in on a Christmas Eve twenty-nine years before, me in my paint coveralls in an echo-y living room bare then of carpet and drapes, like the fir in the corner, projects arrayed like packages, my still-little family asleep, me young and able, working into the night alone with possibility and preparation, listening in some very happy region to the joy indeed and to "Beautiful Savior" on our old portable hi-fi.

That Saturday morning, "Jingle Bells" and "It's Beginning to Look a Lot like Christmas" sent me frayed and rumpled downstairs for stashed goods in the storage room piled with girls' wedding gifts still waiting for places to live. The light seemed too dim and me too short to tell which boxes were full of old ornaments and which of new. Always someone else had rummaged and reached, pulled down and carried up to me balls or demitasse and miniatures to boughs, the stockings to mantel, the crèche to prominence. Now my cheek, injured that summer before, hurt bending down, and my back, fused fourteen years ago, ached carrying up.

The record that flopped onto the others to invite the wobbly needle was the Jay Welch Chorale singing "Do You Hear What I Hear?" Marilyn Wood, my crazy, wonderful friend, was singing on it, the last gift she and Dick brought to our door the Christmas before she died of cancer six and a half years ago.

I set down the carton of Santa mugs with their eyes washed away after twenty-five years of hot chocolate, and attacked the job of balancing the cookie tree and its twelve days of Christmas as Johnny Mathis and "I'll Be Home for Christmas" told me that Megan, our youngest, could not be home this year and nothing anywhere was the same.

I sat at the kitchen table strewn with Christmas lists and empty places and let despair flood me with tears. I was sixty-two and coming back to life excruciatingly different from a year ago, let alone from five, twenty, or from thirty-seven years before when on the twenty-seventh of December I had been a bride off to California with a new husband and a life full of every kind of promise.

Seven months earlier, in May, that now-older husband had had heart surgery, a triple bypass. One day we were playing tennis and he was short of breath; two days later an angiogram showed his left main artery 95 percent occluded. At any moment, he could have had a heart attack that most certainly would have been fatal. But he was saved. By making some changes, big ones, not only in those arteries, which someone else changed for him, but in his diet, and his way of life.

When he was barely recovered, just before the Fourth of July, I'd had my encounter with a crowbar that crashed through the windshield into my face and temple, barely missing my eye. I was riding along the freeway with our son-in-law Jim, returning from camping with his family and Mel—Mel's first outdoor adventure since his heart surgery. Suddenly, my whole life changed. That crash, a split in the windshield, my hand full of blood, eight fractures in my face, temple, jaw. No one believing that I could have survived. Plastic surgeons put together the eight fractures around my eye and in my cheek, temple, and jaw, using screws and plates, most of the surgery done through my mouth to avoid scarring. But scarring was the least of my concerns. I wanted to be alive and able to see. And to be around, with my family and those precious others, for a lot of July Fourths and Christmases to come.

So this was one heck of a way to start spending a day, let alone the whole Christmas season, maybe forever, feeling sorrier for myself than I ever could remember. I felt drowned in deprivation, victimized by time. I hated it.

As usual, it was people who saved me. I wrestled myself to the phone, found a dear friend dying to put up someone else's tree, as she never liked to for herself in her house alone. I called oldest grandkids Nick and Richard, twelve and ten, offered eggnog and the fun of hanging ornaments from Siberia before emptying the Ping-Pong table for a game.

In half an hour all of us were humming "Rudolph" and "Away in a Manger" as we scurried new candles into old holdings and scolded reluctant light clips onto prickly branches.

Of course there was not enough time. They had to leave, and I had to meet a man at my studio to fix my ailing computer printer. We left a terrible mess of straw from the manger, unusable bows, boxes to be loaded back downstairs, the half-arranged tree skirt and stockings. But it was all right. All that could be cleared up easily. We had launched the present season, and they had saved me from the past.

But more than that had happened. By evening, when I had been at my keyboard working, even half seeing, on *Russia*, a two-and-a-half-year, five-hundred-page project, had taken time to be alone in a fashion that made sense, I came back to the mess cleared up by Mel, home in late afternoon from his meeting and keyed up by it for new ways to operate his business and his life. He'd always helped, with changing diapers, wringing out floods, making Christmas happen. Despite his busyness away from it, that home has never been anything but very much his too, and he has attended me with loving regard and companionship. But time had stalked his moments there like a starving tiger. And, born of his parents' depression mold, fear—of depletion.

We talked about change, aging, and spending, mostly about the shutters in the living room that I had ordered and put up without his knowing—a total switch in the way we had always managed. We have very different ideas about spending at any age, always have had. He wants to have money to save; I figure resources are to spend, personal or monetary. And my father's motto, "Things work out," also out of the depression, had kept me buoyant even in days when we were too student poor to own a stove with an oven.

Now we are in a new place and time. And we'd better look at how we expect to spend ourselves on it before it spends us into depletion and tears. We must each do what we do and be who we are, alone as well as together, or growing old in the same household could be like the pulling of blinds for one or the other—or both.

I have always recognized that, thanks to Mel and his ways of earning and saving, I am a privileged woman, never needing to work for financial security, only for the wholeness in the working. And the luxury of having earnings that I can spend for surprises like a snowblower—a welcome convenience given his ailing back

—or a cabin on the mountain or shutters for the living room. More, I have had the health and energy to work hard at home to earn that prerogative of working wherever else demand and fancy have taken me. Meanwhile, we both—and the household—have benefitted in my being able to operate mostly from home, thanks to Mel. Now we sidle into a new era.

No, I will not have children to decorate with, nor my committee of daughters to cook with, nor a husband, well but nervous even in a time of plenty and semi-retirement, not headed out the door to the office. Neither will I have the litheness to go for the low boxes or branches. And certainly I can't expect a return in anything but memory of other capacities and dears from a past I so adore.

What I have now is a life I have waited far too long to harness, given me indeed by Grace. What I can do is what I can do best, what I have learned about from all those 62 years—using my head and my heart and my fingers where my strength and circumstances and even temporary incapacity will no longer let me. Gratefully and without guilt. Yes, even with a lovely modicum of serenity in the means and joy of finally being free to choose.

Of course I can cook if I want to, or put up a tree, or clear up a mess. Goodness knows I've served my apprenticeships, have loved the serving and the learning how. But I realize I'm simply accepting now what I've raced toward every day of that other lifetime—a chance to be the self that has waited to come alive.

Beyond that, after my accident, when I couldn't read, work, or put my face down for seven months, I learned to listen to a distant music, to pay attention as I never had to the divine in humanness. I had been to another home and had returned. I wanted a life trimmed and useful in new ways. What I had to give was different from what it had been. And the same had to be true for Mel.

Unlike a woman in her home, Mel and my brothers have the right to retire from offices and labs, not to take on what they did at thirty-five or even fifty. All too often women are expected—or, more truly, we expect it of ourselves—still to be playing in that playhouse we fashioned in our twenties. Only with no dolls to be put to bed, and yet the routines that included the dolls to be continued.

Time is short and days precious. This Christmas season I will not do things the same as I always have. I will spend myself more on ideas and promulgating them than on open-face sandwiches and distributing them. Peace on earth, good will to all must be more than a Christmas bromide. "And let it begin with me" must be in my heart and in my home if peace is to be a valid concern anywhere else in my life or my world. That peace must be part of everything I am in on. Yes, even in a lovely modicum of serenity —of faith and having enough to give away.

I will have more of my grandchildren one at a time to talk and spree with than in hordes to try to get through to. Not that I would ever want to miss the celebrations or catastrophes, no matter the size, that involve my people. But I will enjoy more time year round with my family and friends without crowding, either in time or numbers, and let that be the gift to both them and me at Christmas.

Most of all, I will enjoy the accessible silence of these years—if the phone doesn't ring—a silence that lets my head loose and my heart find its way to new settlings that I realize I've waited too long to explore.

Grateful for the resources and the inclination, I would like to stay solvent by spending myself on what is yet to come. It just may be the only way to grow older without growing old. After all, at sixty-two, what in this world do I want to save for?

Today I am young again, intrigued by a future that tells me, regardless of anything, that I would not go back a finger's worth. Not even for a Christmas like those in our home movies that we never seem to have time, even on video now, to see all the way through. I like now. And I like that Mel is able to be a new part of now, to enjoy as he never has the fruits of his so eloquent labors over the years. Life is just beginning for both of us.

And I love the privilege of getting to be in on it alive and almost well—and wiser by far than I was thirty-seven years or even twenty-four hours ago.

Come home for Christmas, everyone who can. Be as always part of me and my house that is not your home as it used to be, any more than it is mine. But oh, how I love it to be filled with you. You'll play your violins, piano, and flute for me; and I'll probably cry as I always have when you play "Danny Boy" and "Silent Night" and "Movin' On." But it will be all right. We'll have a just fine time together—and apart. And not one tear will be for what waits out there for all of us—a new year and a new way to go. As I'm very certain it was meant to be.
(Adapted from original in *Network*, December 1987, and *Exponent II*, Winter 1987.)

The Unmistakable Ever

The most he ever did or does
    is love her.
The least, be spare with life,
    his wardrobe of loose hung
    browns and blues
    not ever to be thrown away.

Because he would not willingly
    choose the new
    he loves the old in her,
    the shrinking reach, the less able legs,
    the body surrendering
    to gravity.
Much that might well be discarded
    he hovers about, kissing
    the creped neck, holding
    the spotted hands, offering
    a lift to the stalled spirits.

Sleep too is spare.
What he spends is nights never his own,

taken by trips to the bathroom,
worries snagged on long-gone deals
with what never came out anything
but good.

And now the unmistakable ever
    of children and 10,000 common
    denominators collects them both
    in the late spending
    of gathering, gathering the bundles
    of daisies that have persisted
    among the sage and dogwood,
    the aspen and insidious morning glory

to wisp white and odorless
    from the old soil, the rotted poles,
    creosoted new thirty years ago
    and laid by them to retain
    the mulch of winter
    and the raking out of spring.

(Poem adapted from original in *Network*,
December 1987, and *Exponent II*,
Winter 1987.)

Afterword

To have had time and reason for meditating on housekeeping and homemaking has been a great privilege. It has supplied me a chance to process the abundance of a season, a decade, a day, a night, to be informed: Not to live by a list mentality, but to afford the right to pay attention. Not to be so bludgeoned by input and activity that life and connectedness to the eternal go unnoticed.

Three years ago, it was my accident that caused me to notice. In surviving that blow of a crowbar through the windshield at sixty-five miles per hour to my face, eye, temple, when survival was simply impossible, I came back to my home from my home. And in seven months of not being able to read or move quickly or even to put my face down to work, I learned to hear an inner music that I know now I had been taught to listen to long before.

I can't help feeling that Mother and Grandma did their share of meditating as they went through their days doing their tasks and shaping the rest of us. I realize that both of them brought more to keeping house than doing their work here upon the earth.

Like with Mother and the barometer. No ordinary barometer, it came across the plains in my great-grandfather's covered wagon and has hung on an outside wall of every home I've lived in. It is infallible, it outguesses satellites, and it falls and rises the opposite of any of its kind. Wind the gold and the black arrows until they are on top of each other, and tap gently. The black arrow goes up toward storm, down toward very dry. The movement, delicate or sudden, foretells the intensity of change. Mother's daily ritual was tapping the barometer and then "working on the weather" for any of us who were traveling.

We grew up watching her stand just below the landing in the hall next to our front door, tapping the barometer with two fingernails. We knew she was checking it for Father. As district manager for Ford Motor Company, he traveled much in our growing up, was out of town more than in. But my brothers and I knew he and Mother were in touch, not only through their daily letters and her long visits on her knees, but through her affinity with the barometer and its portendings. We had absolute though unspoken faith in Mother's connections.

As we grew into traveling ourselves, as all four of us have been led to do in our chosen professions, Mother tapped the trusty barometer and worked on any weather to let our traveling be always safely back home. We never doubted the still, sure thoughtfulness, the constant prayer that emanated from her and expected a certain return. It permeated our conceptions of then, now, and forever. It was a big part of what made home a safe place.

How she kept her house throbs still in my memory and in how I keep mine, and I hope in how my daughters will keep theirs. That I choose to do it differently has nothing to do with the pulse of what she really taught me: How she regarded her right to tap the barometer and keep in touch. That breathes in me her faith that says, All is well, all is well.

If, in the years of these meditations and many others, I have acquired a little more of her kind of paying attention, I say thank you. And Grandma, Mother, Father, I'm sure you know my traveling is often hectic, haphazard, and self-styled, as it's always been—and often on the wild horse. But it is always toward home. Expecting, expecting, expecting the same welcome and adventure as awaits all the others who are part of me and my house. All of us with lots of places yet to go, traveling and coming home as you taught us to—with love, Mother.

The Right

> This is my actual life. Good midday,
> into which I emerge as the girl on my knees
> (both working!) beside the creek
> pulling away the moss to nuzzle

somewhere in June
or the syllables on a page
coming up with surprise
like what is out from the pine mulch of snow
when this May says it's time.

Beyond any of that, of course, the dreams,
all that persists after sleep
and before waking, under the blue canyon quilt,
staying warm all over
like being closer to Finally!

Holding without holding onto my loves—
so much more than allotted by even
a lifetime of new leaves
and the embellishments of fall air
and the dear detail of faces,
the smell of under a rock,
and the unblemished news of small fingers.

This is the very thing on the way
to where it was headed with that girl:
the meadow by Lovers' Lane
where fairy tales and visions blundered
into each other and chose this place

that is close, close to all the trees
caressing the sky with a hole in it
to the other place
where the girl is right with
the still-to-be things in the stillness
of when light goes on

and love calls kindness back to life
because it is right
like the sound of water beside a story
that says exactly what it was meant to say.